Rhythm -n- Hues

The Adult Coloring Book with Soul

eLIZabeth d. schafer

Dedication

I'd like to dedicate my first book to my family. You provided me love and support throughout the years, but also encouraged me to dream without limitations. Yet you never forced me to fit in the box or color inside the lines. You helped me gain the confidence to realize that with hard work I could achieve anything, and that it was acceptable to be different which allowed me to grow into my own uniqueness. Our beginnings were humble, and even though we couldn't afford the big box of 64 crayons; I certainly dreamed in all those marvelous colors. Finally, most humbly and with love I say to all of you…

Thank you.

Liz
Author and Illustrator

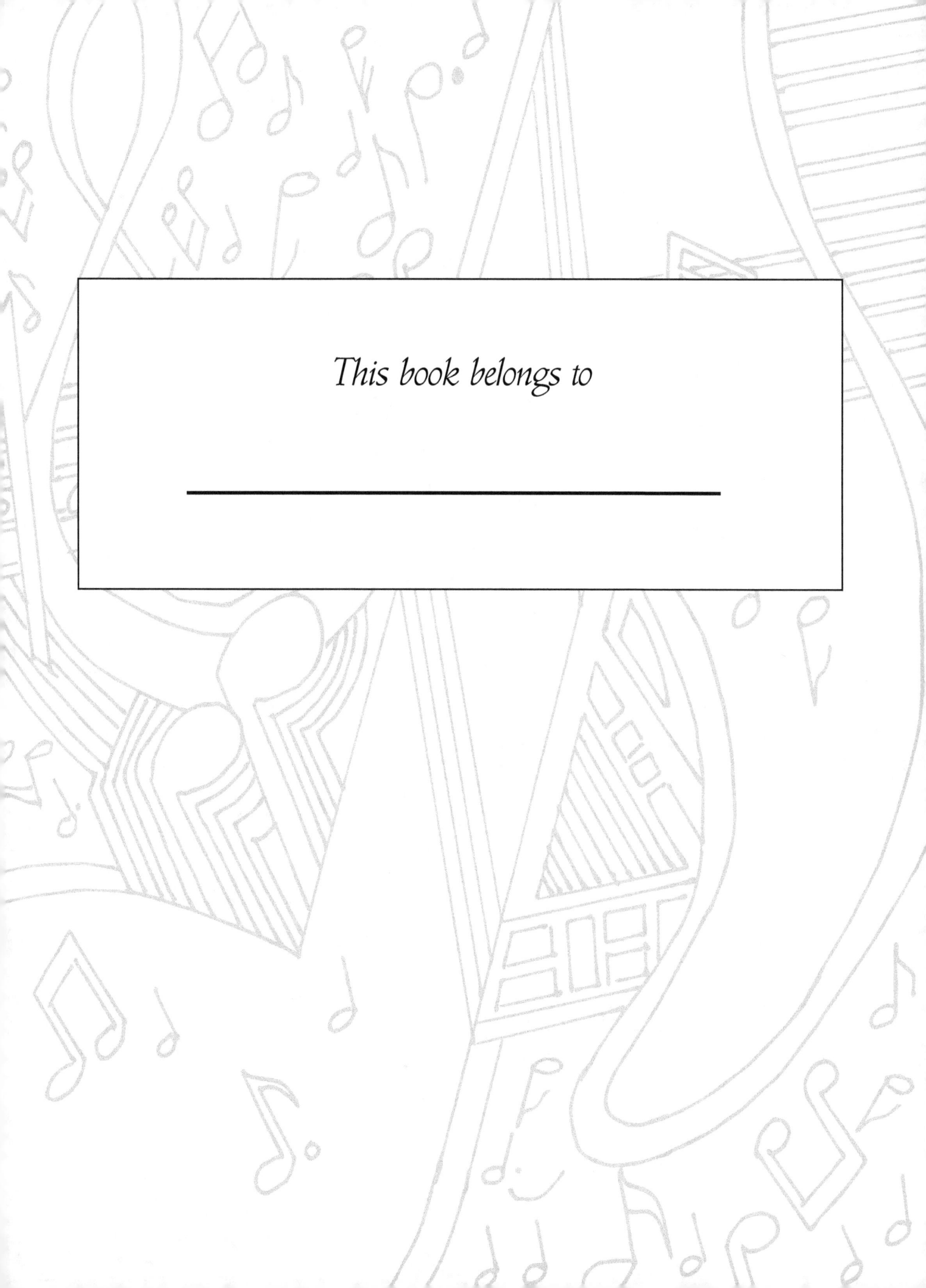

This book belongs to

Introduction

Music and art have been a driving force throughout my life, and combining both of these passions into a series of artworks has been a natural extension of me. The illustrations in this book were formed from the pure joy I experience with the sound and rhythm of music.

I gained a greater understanding and appreciation of music after moving to the south. In New Orleans, the birth place of jazz, and Mississippi, the birth place of blues, music envelops life; and here I find a huge well of inspiration from spending numerous nights at music clubs and concerts, dancing and sketching the music.

This coloring book has soul; it's a coloring book through an artist's eyes with some inter-mingling of my philosophies on life. The images are stylized hand-drawn illustrations. All were inspired from my original sketches that were used for my painting series of instruments, drawn during long nights in the music clubs and painted during long days in the studio all while dancing across my canvas to the music. In revisiting these sketches for "Rhythm –n- Hues" I see that they are still vibrant works and must live on to provide a new conversation in a different, more personal way. Several of these illustrations are new designs created just for you. I've even included some unfinished illustrations and blank pages for you to add your own ideas and doodles. All of which are waiting to be brought to life with your unique ideas and color.

Coloring provides a rhythmic motion, and if done for an extended period of time becomes a meditation. Here you can find an inner peace if you create alone or connect with friends in parallel play with coloring parties. However, coloring books aren't just a static entity meant for coloring as they may also be a jumping off point for creative inspiration.

I'd love to see where these illustrations take you, along with getting your feedback. Therefore, I want to encourage you to share your colored creations by posting on Facebook.com/liz.artbyliz and Instagram/ ArtbyLiz_Studio #rhythmnhuescolor.

I want you to set your creativity free! Put on your favorite music and play with color.

Enjoy! Liz

Coloring Tips

1. *Pull out your crayons, colored pencils, or markers. Maybe all 3…whatever works for you.*

2. *No image in this book is exact, as it is hand-drawn by me. As such, you should add your own creative touch as there is no "perfect way" to color.*

3. *Turn off your phone, tablet, computer, and television (any distractions).*

4. *Don't know where to start? Pick your favorite image, no matter if it's in the middle, beginning or end, and start there.*

5. *Cool colors (such as blue, green, and purple) are considered to have calming qualities; while warmer colors (red, orange, and yellow) have more active qualities. Bright colors impart more energy and dark colors reflect a lower energy.*

6. *Have a coloring party with friends and share the experience.*

7. *Put on your favorite music and play.*

8. *Use a blotter page (heavy-weight paper) and place behind your image while you color in order to prevent bleed-through onto other surfaces and to also provide a better surface to enhance your coloring experience.*

9. *All images in the coloring book are single-sided for your ease in framing should you choose.*

10. *Finally, but MOST importantly, relax, escape from the problems of the day and let the world fade away; free your inner creativity and color.*

Let the color wash over you and drown the blues.

Southern Crossroads

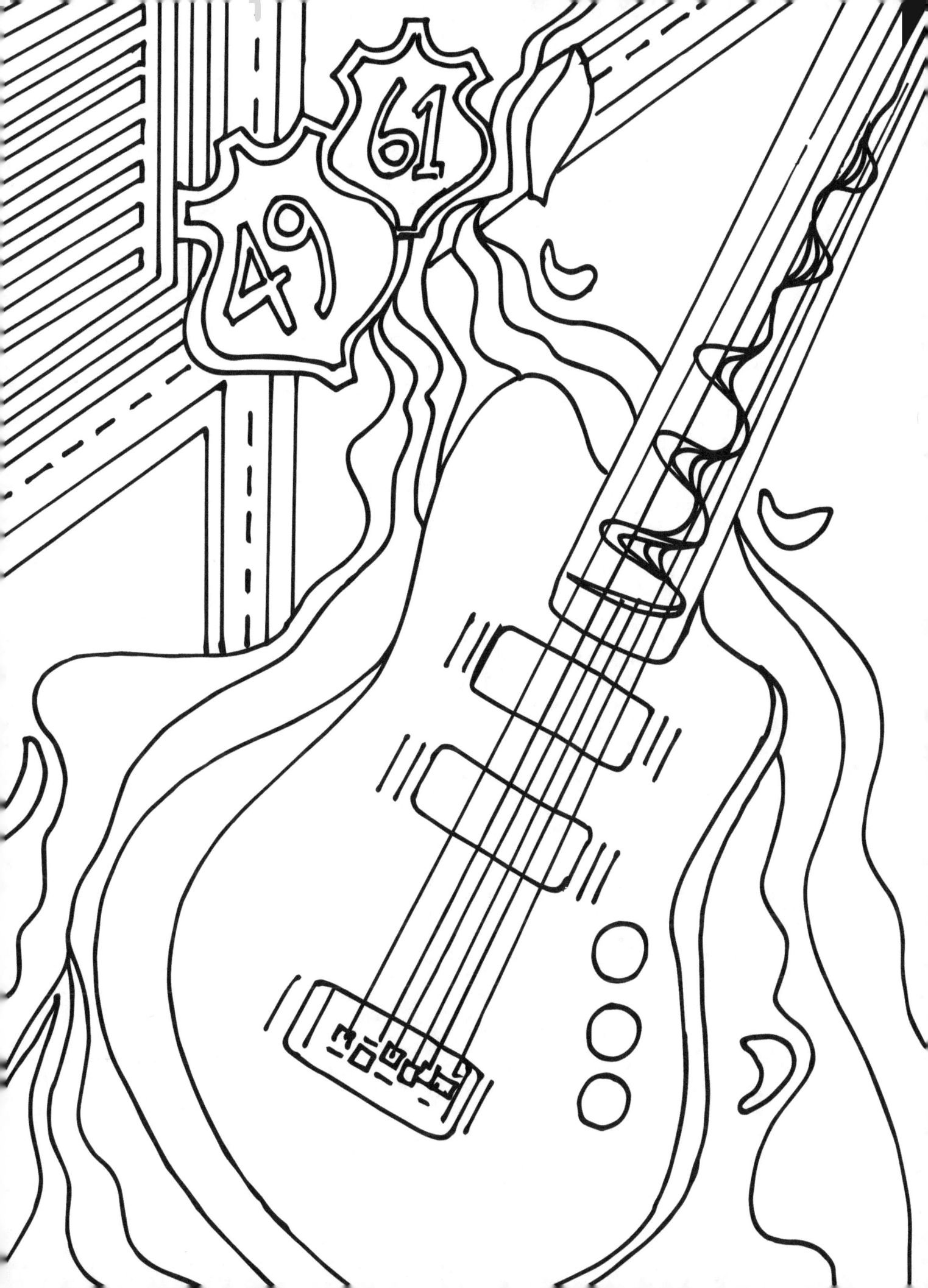

Silence is as important as sound.

Layin' Down Tracks

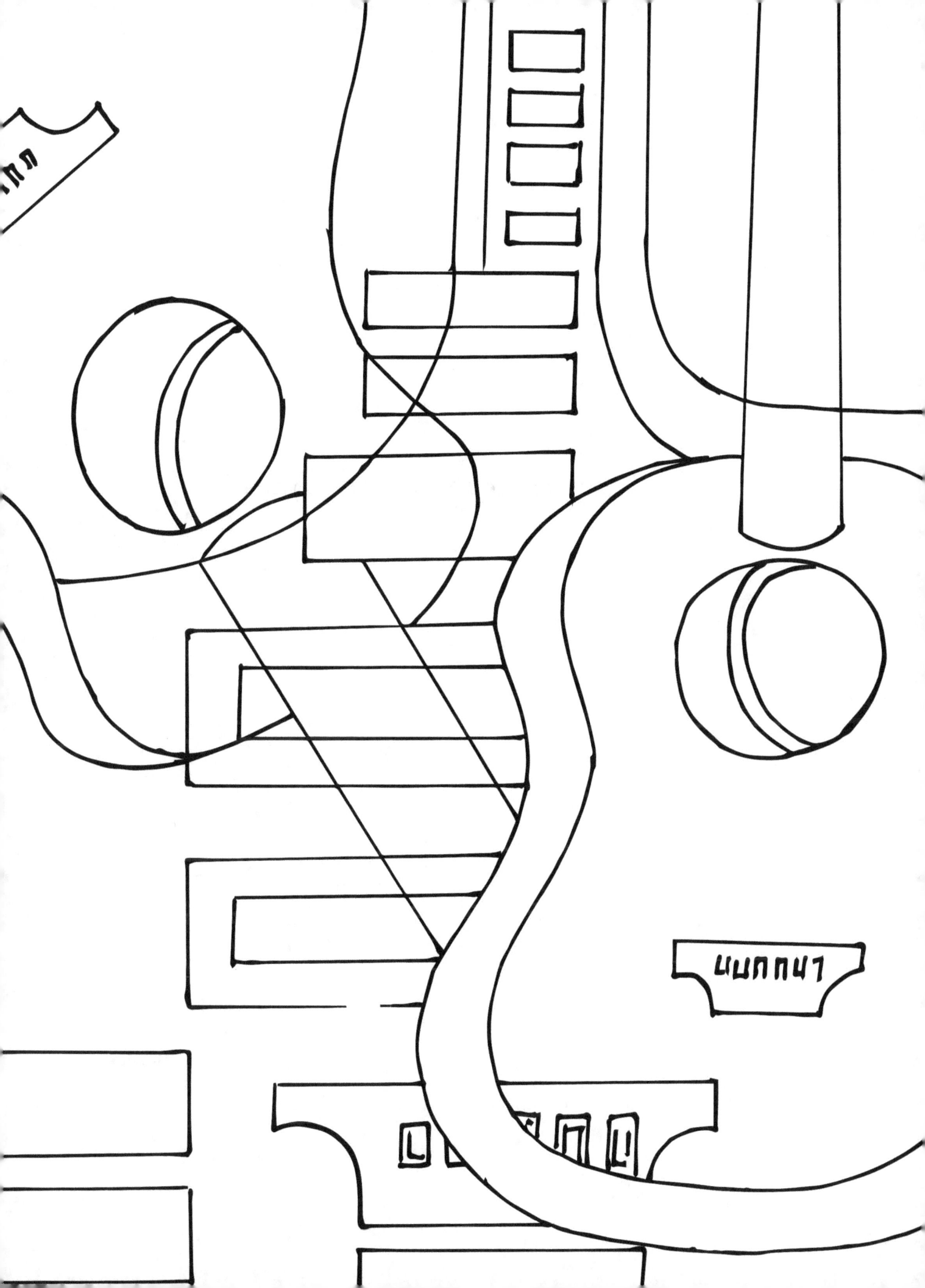

Be present in the moment. Listen to yourself.

Acoustic Trio

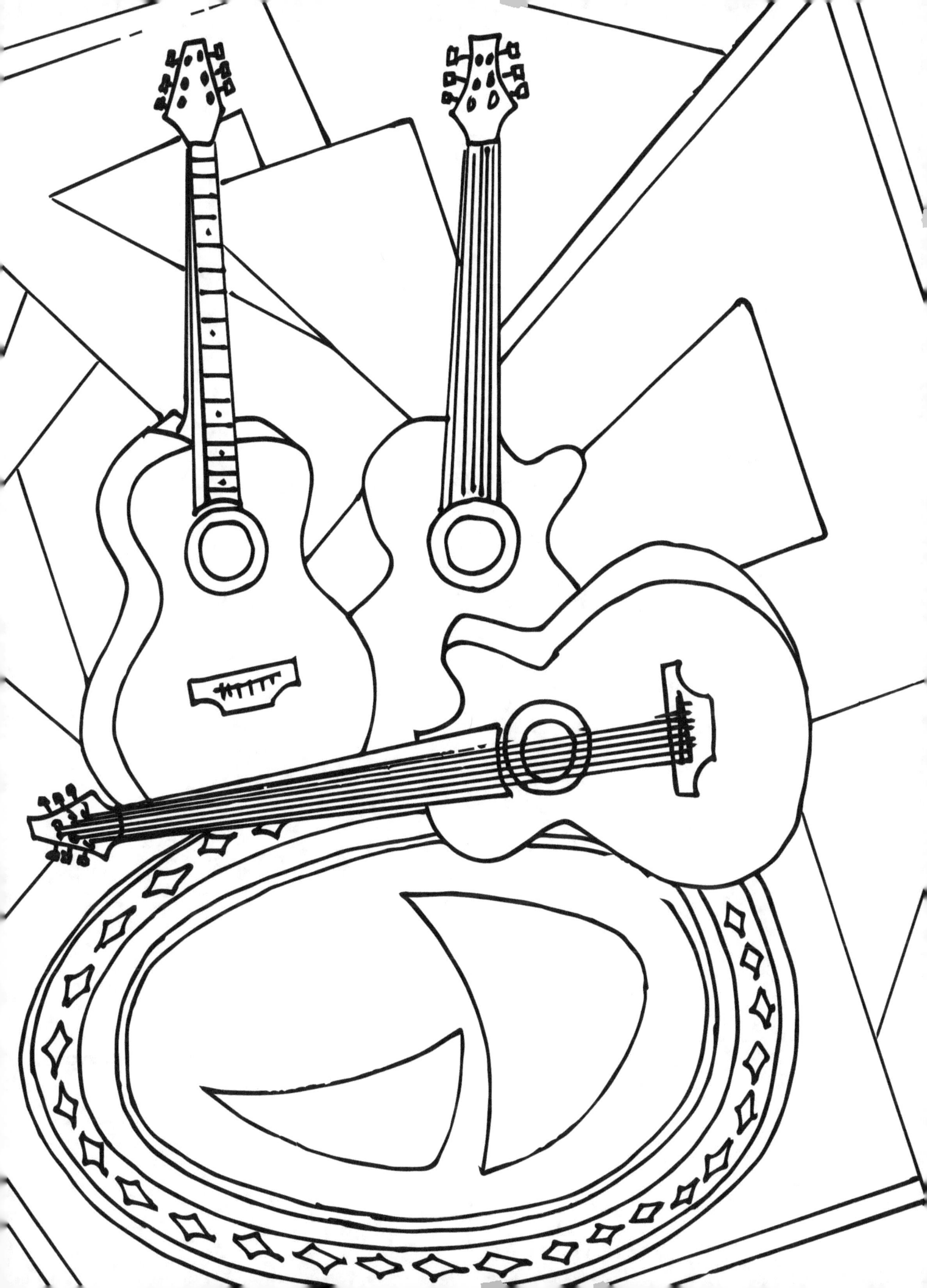

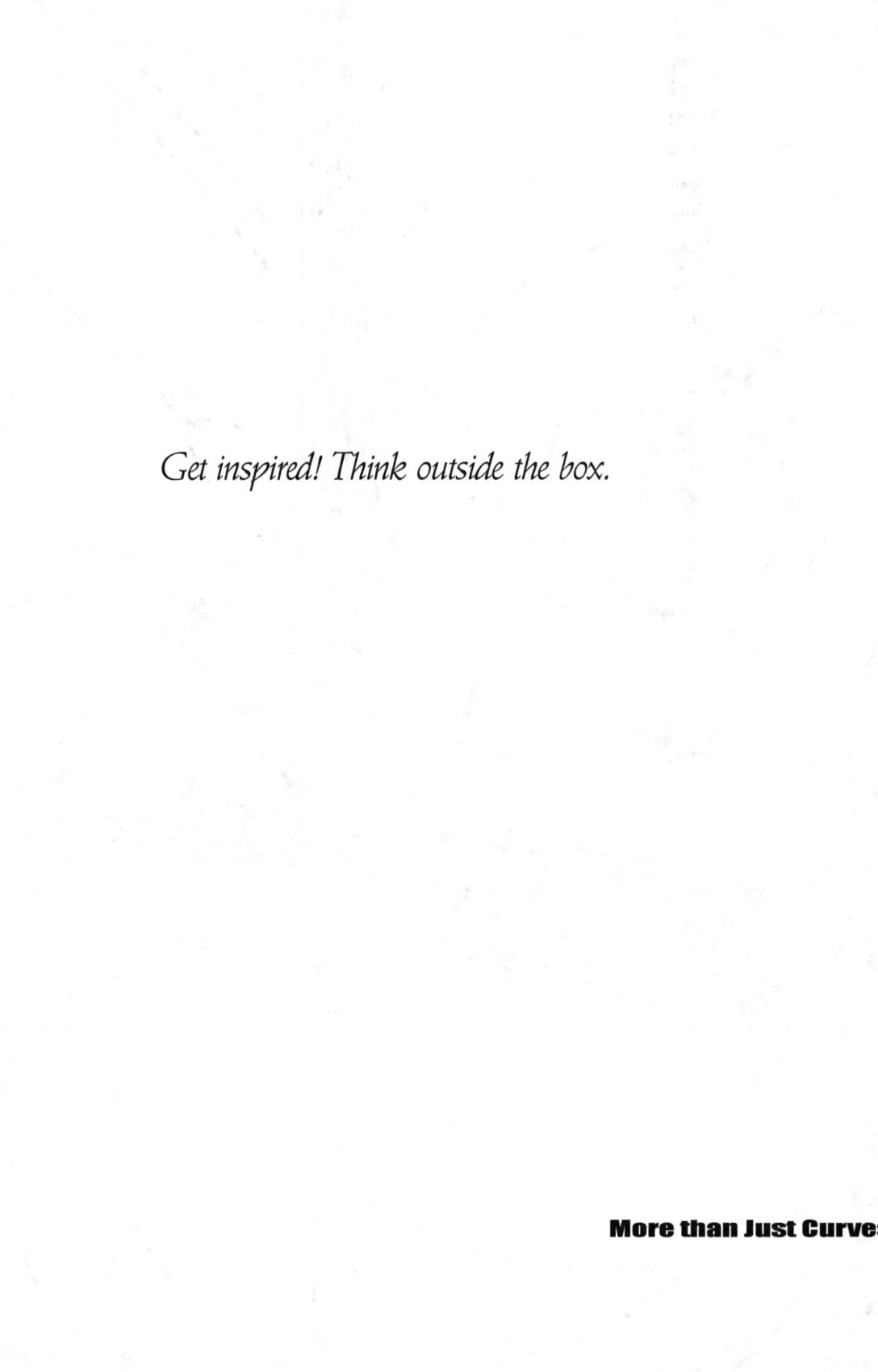

Get inspired! Think outside the box.

More than Just Curves

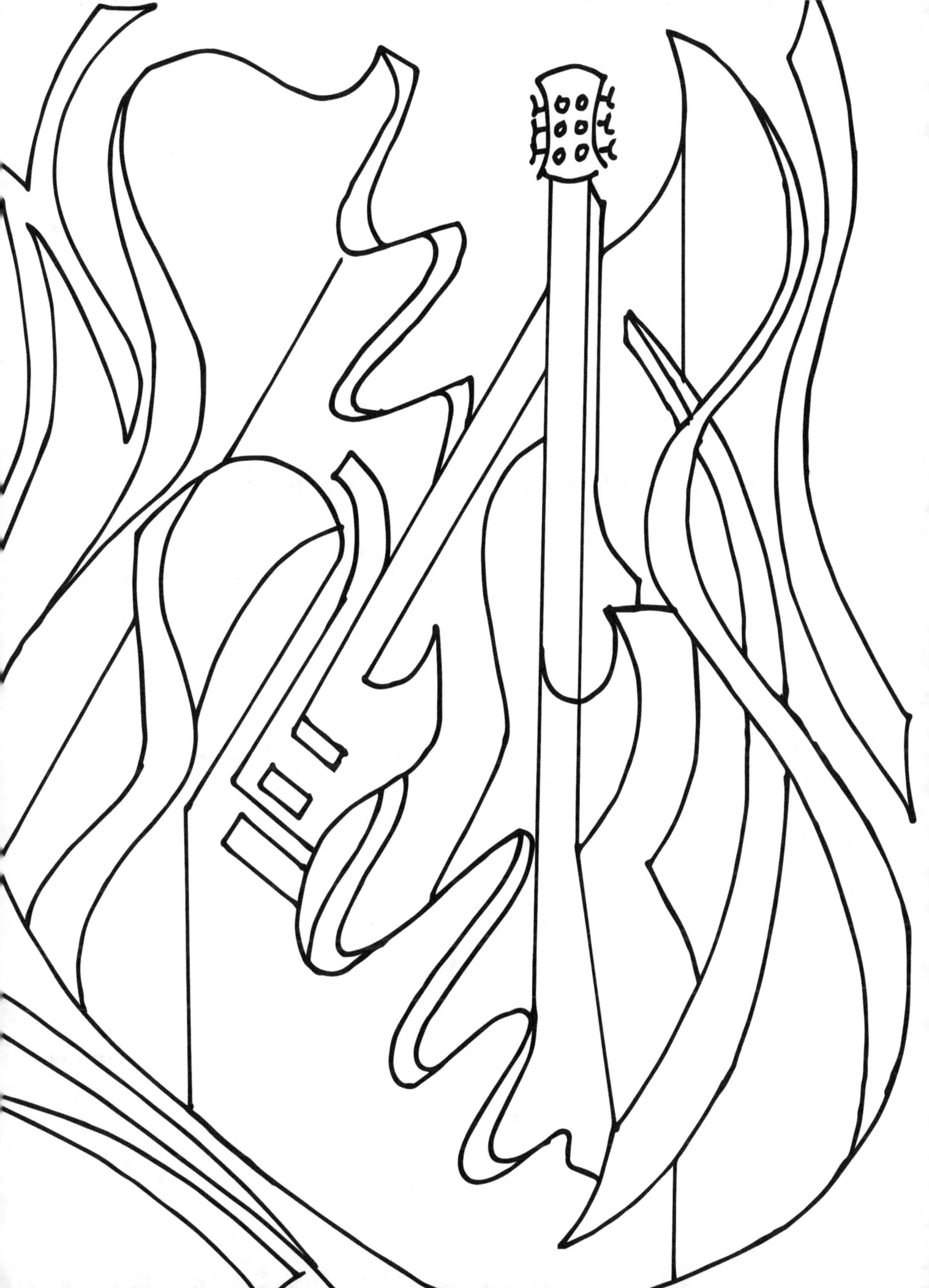

Dance to the rhythms of life instead of running from them.

Tambourines

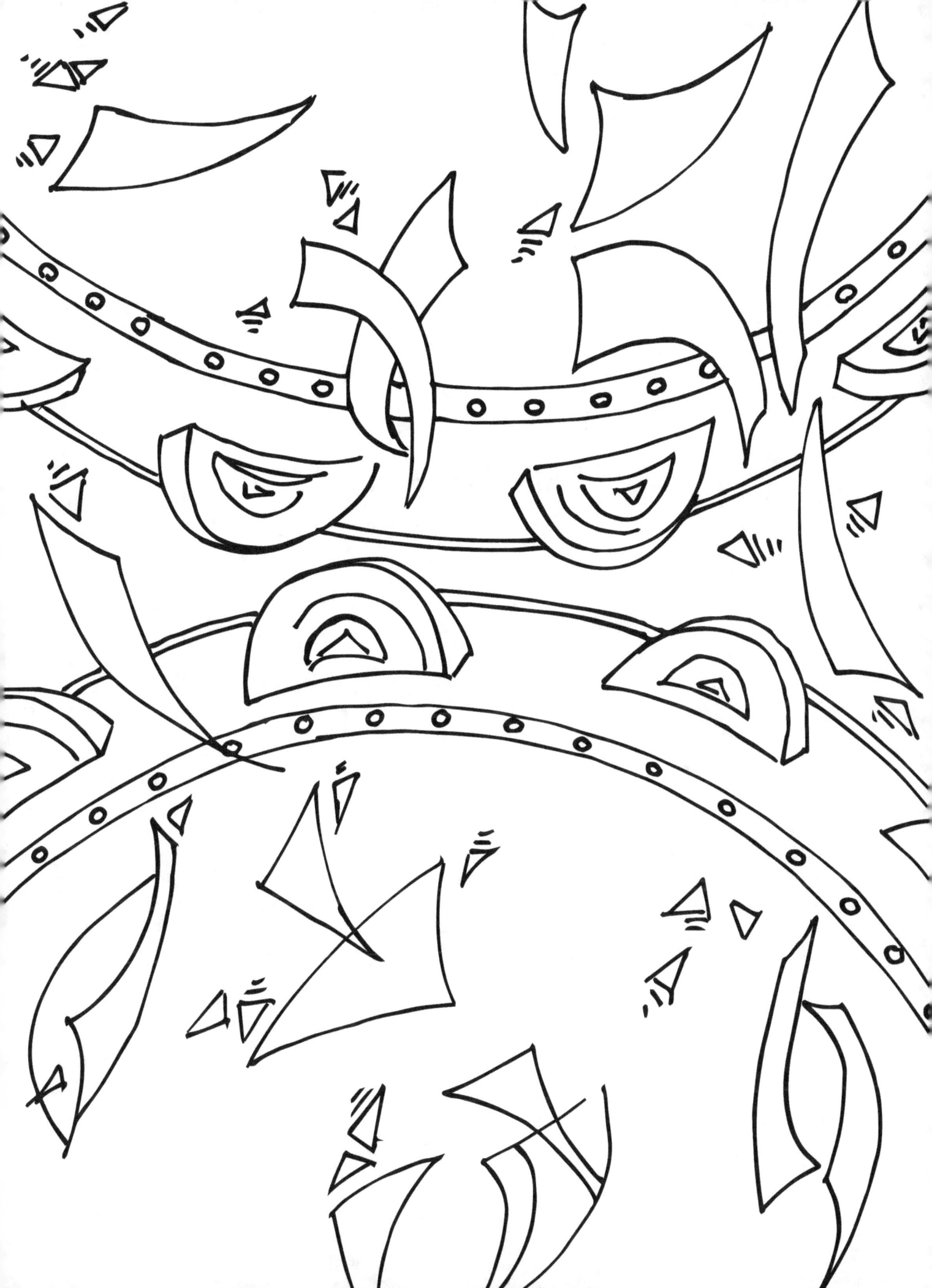

Perform every action artfully.

High Hat

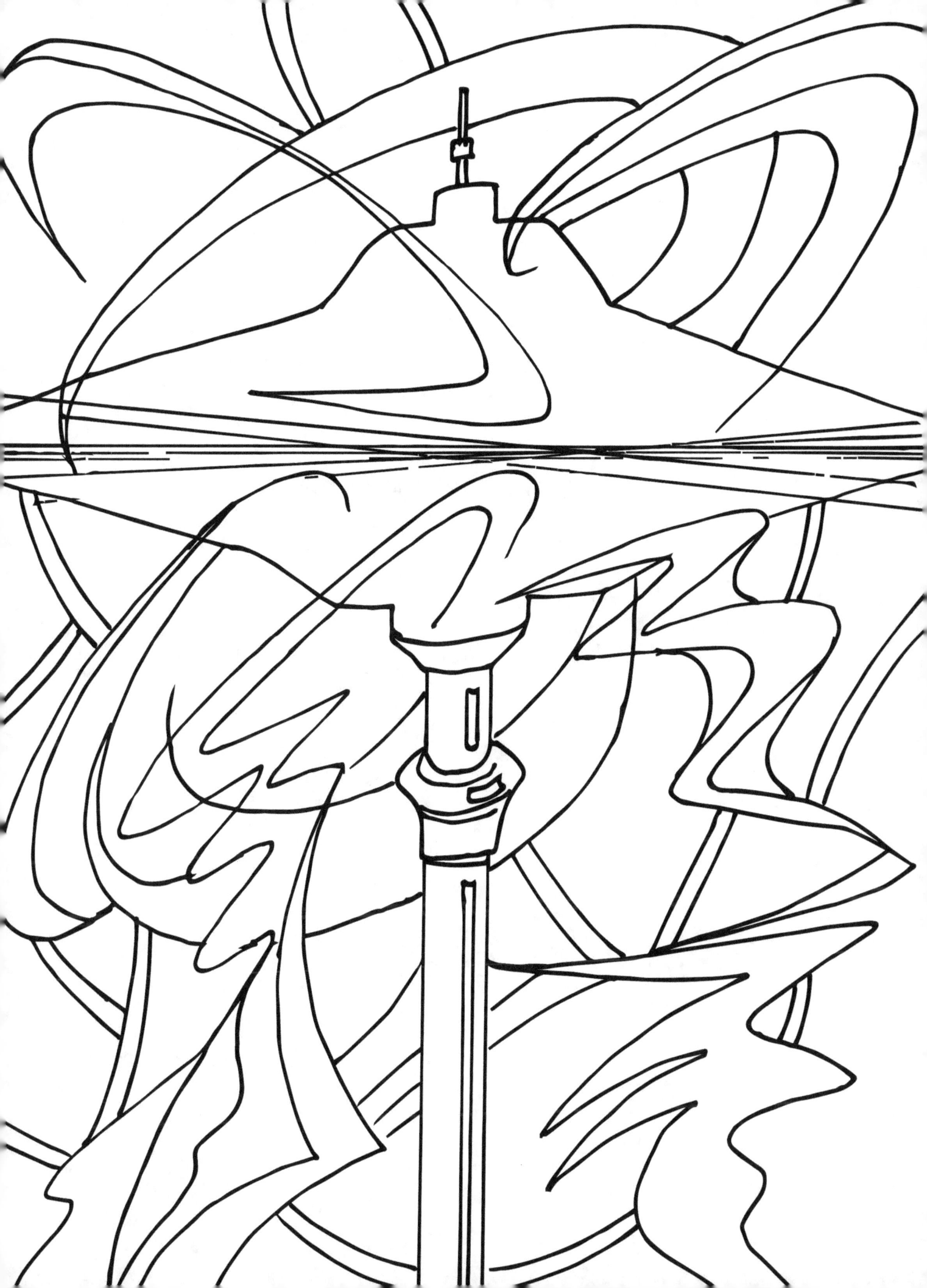

If a crayon drops, who will hear it?

Circle of Cymbals

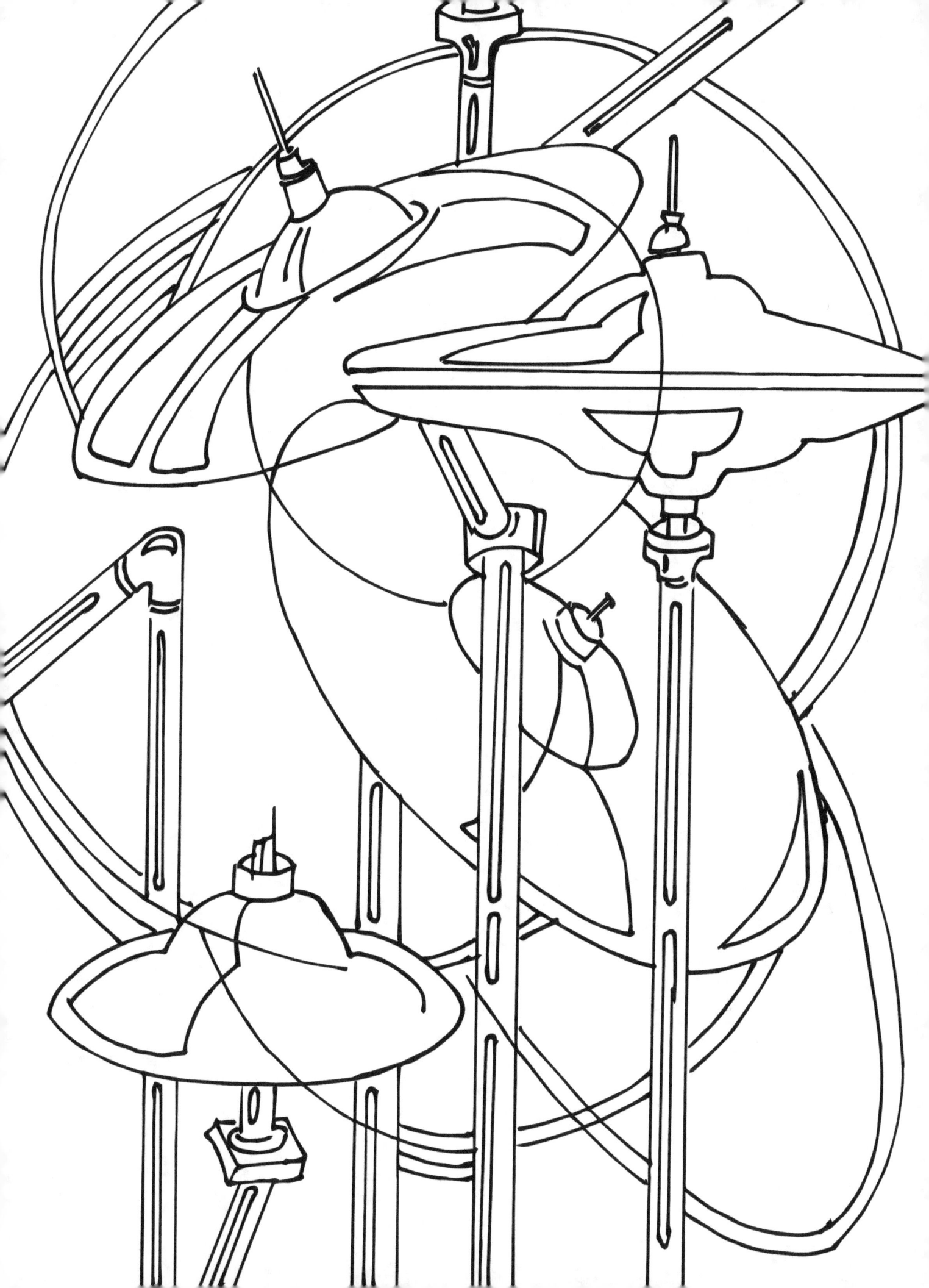

The meaning of music is to tell a story. The reason for art is to tell a story.

Pipe Dreams

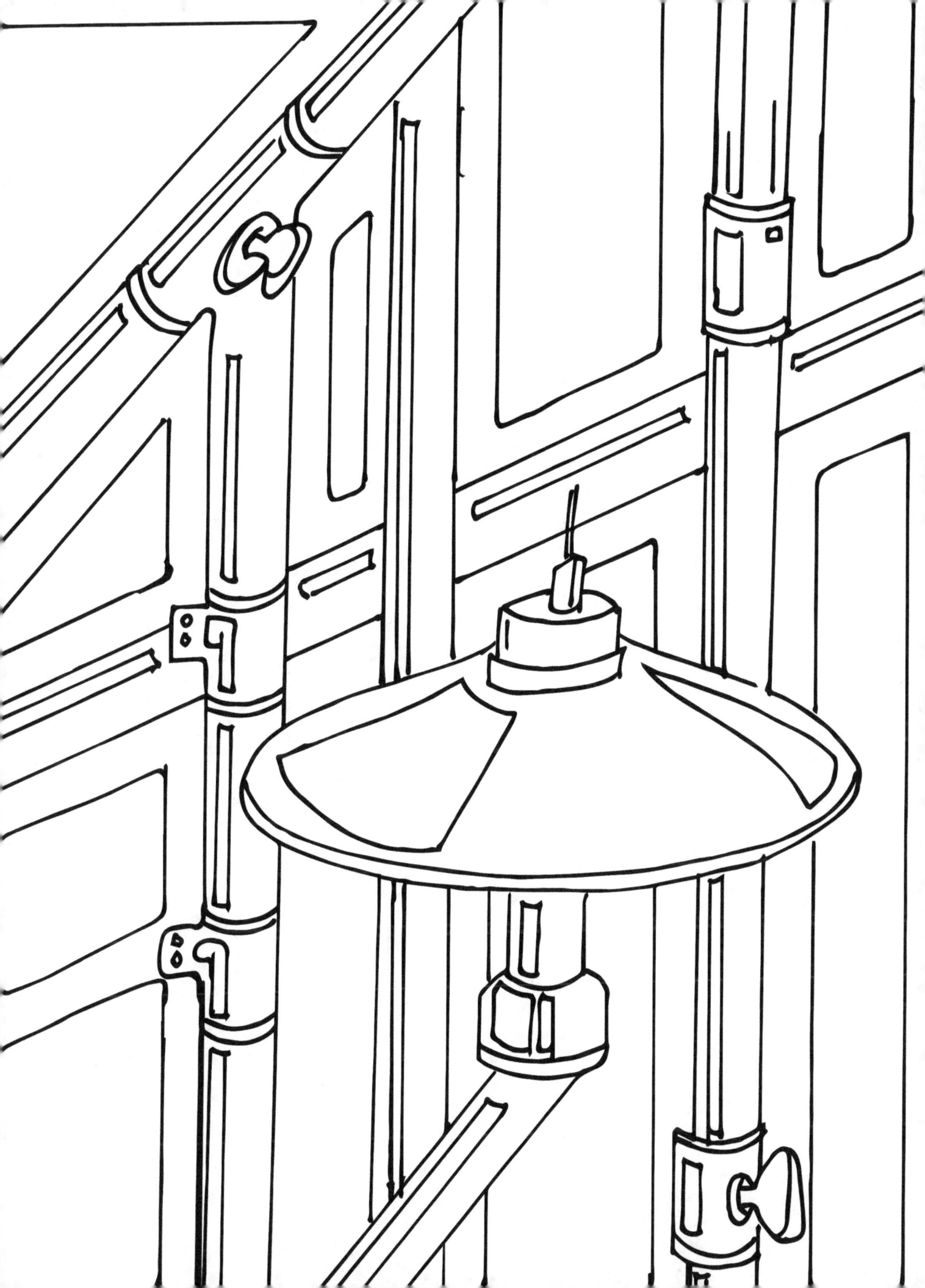

Color with love.

What a Pair

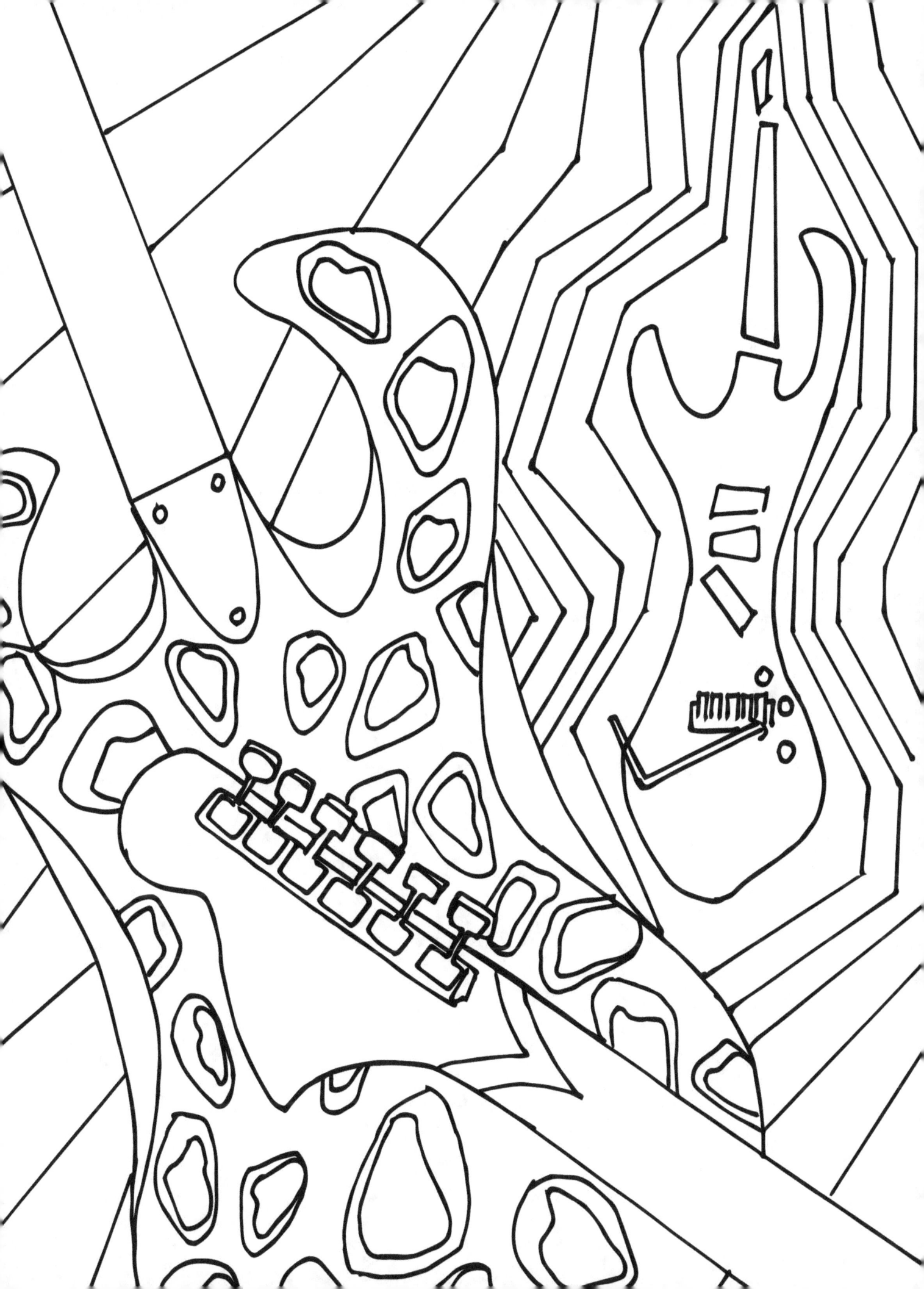

What music do you hear while coloring?

Jam On

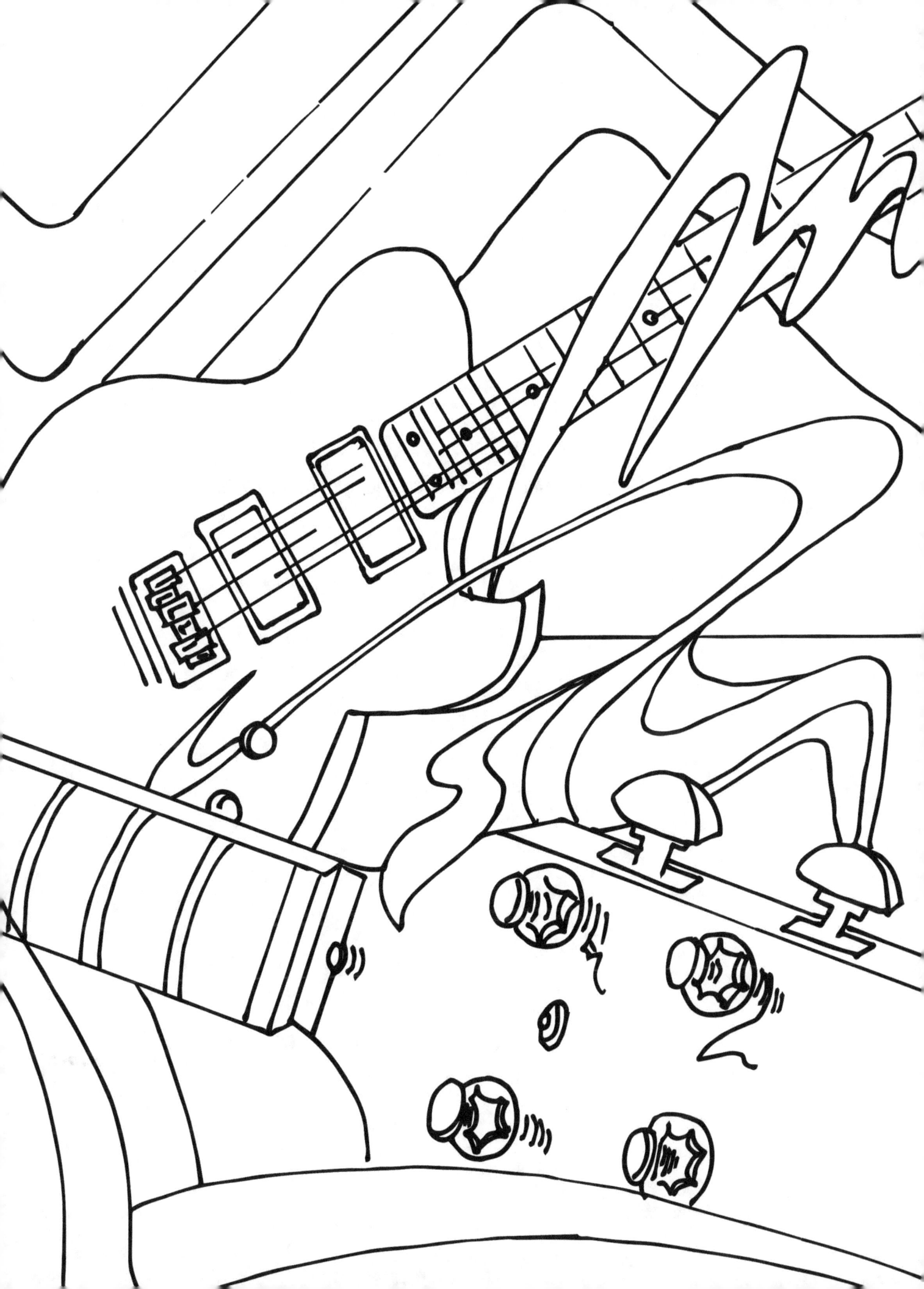

Open the door to experiencing the joy of color.

Tambourine Timbre

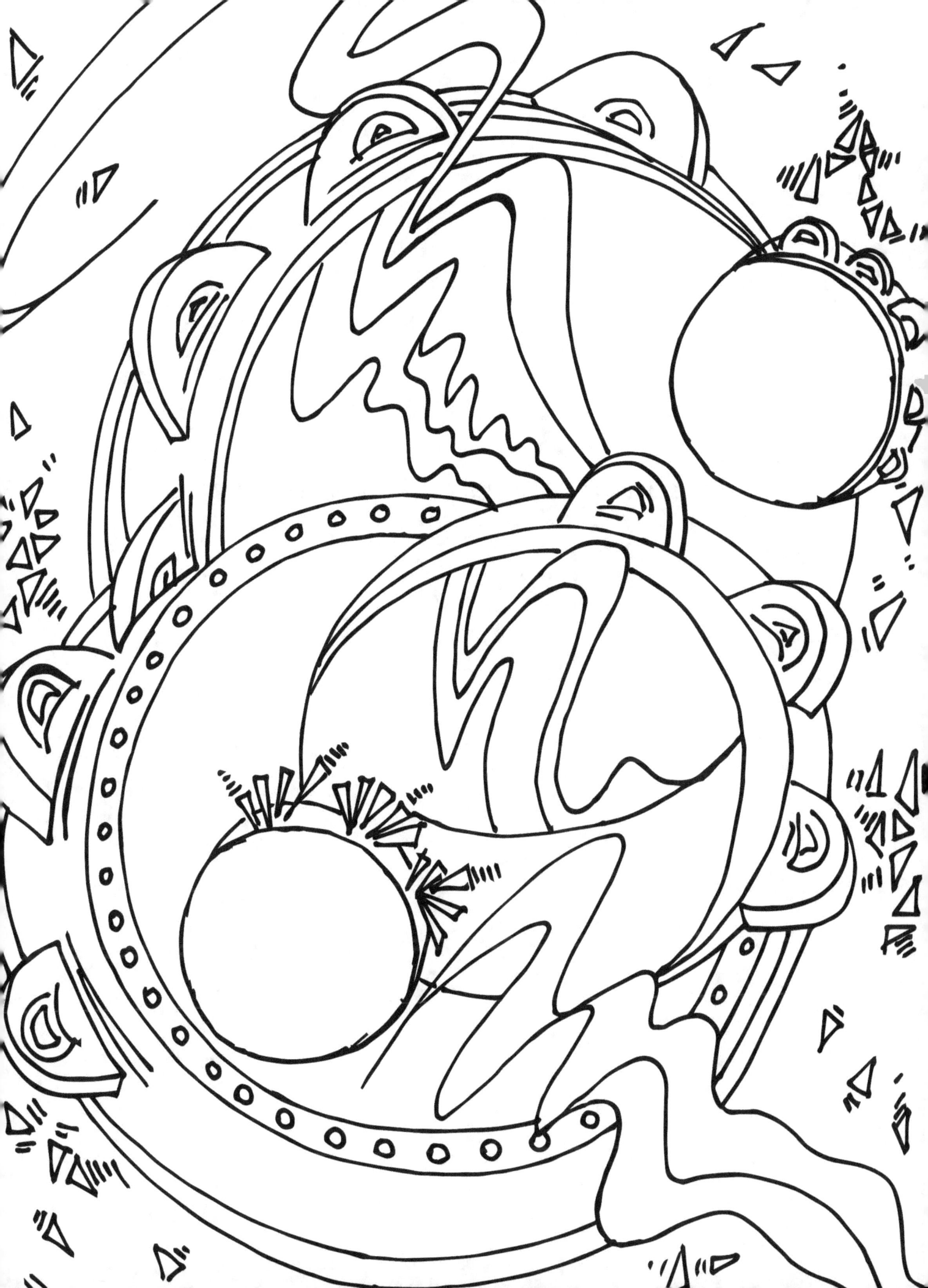

Pretend you are on a tropical beach with the music playing...

Percussion Beats

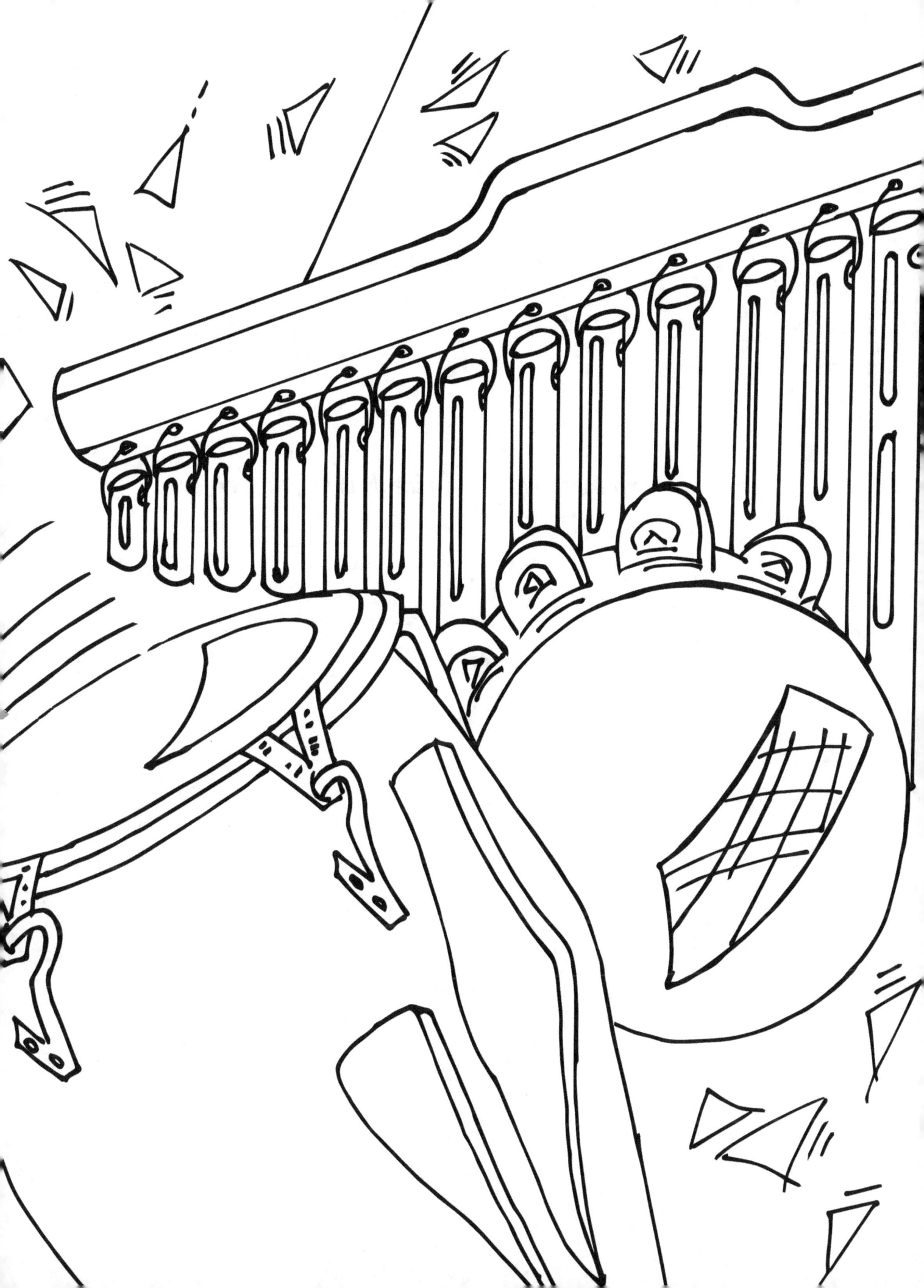

Feel the connection with the rhythms you color.

Exotic Beats

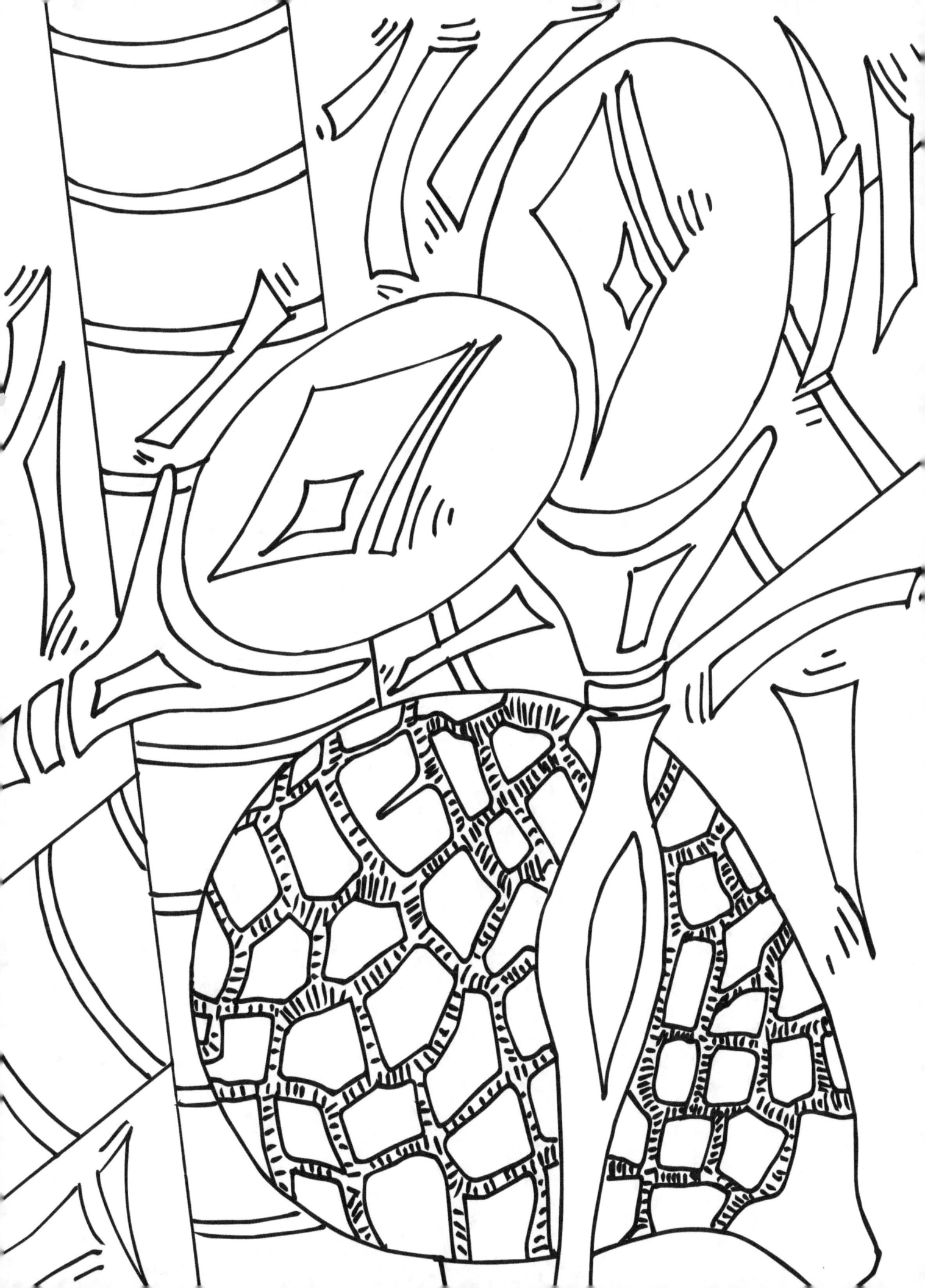

Harmonious sound can be magical.

Dueling Pianos

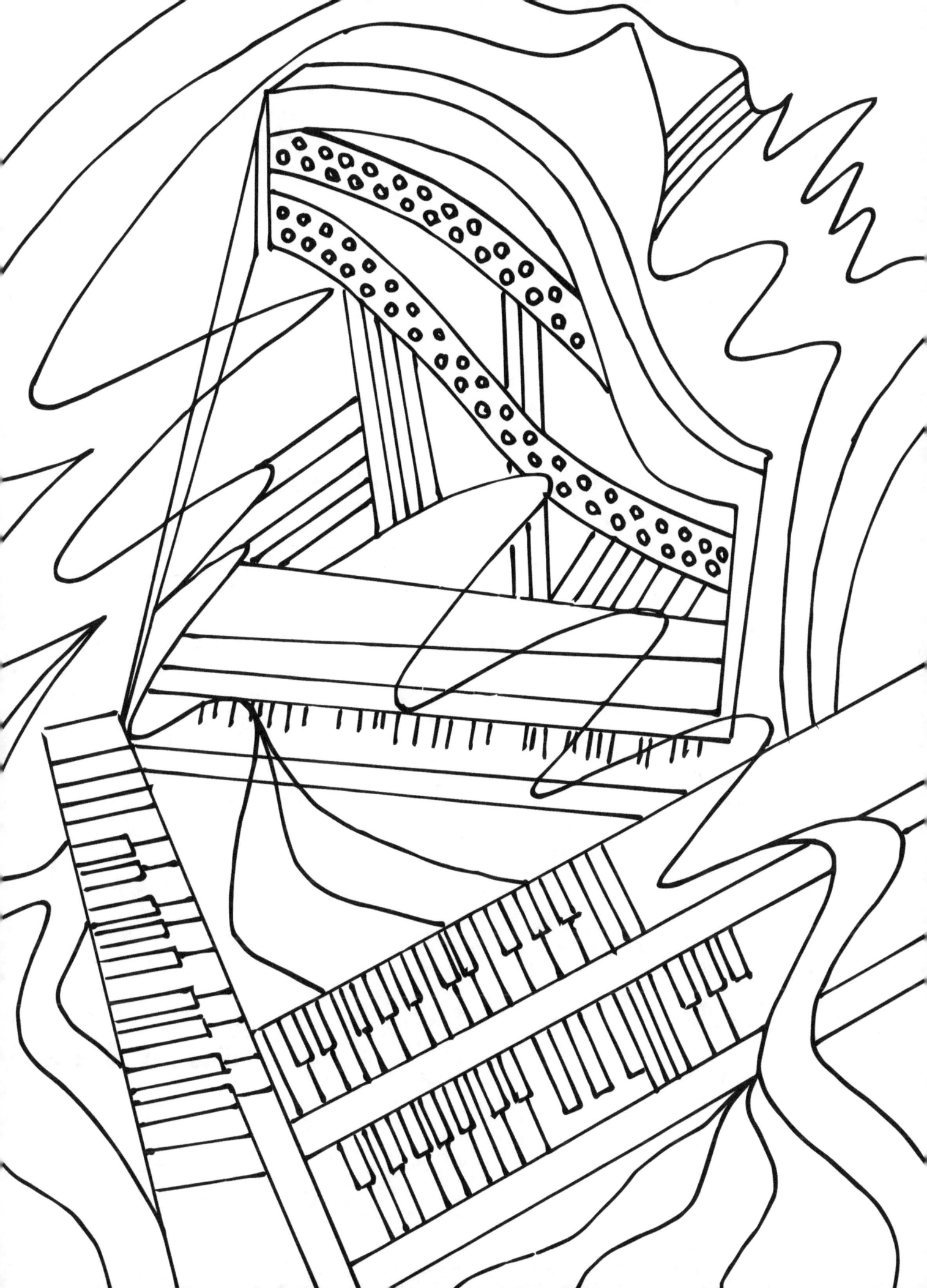

Reflect on the hues of each moment.

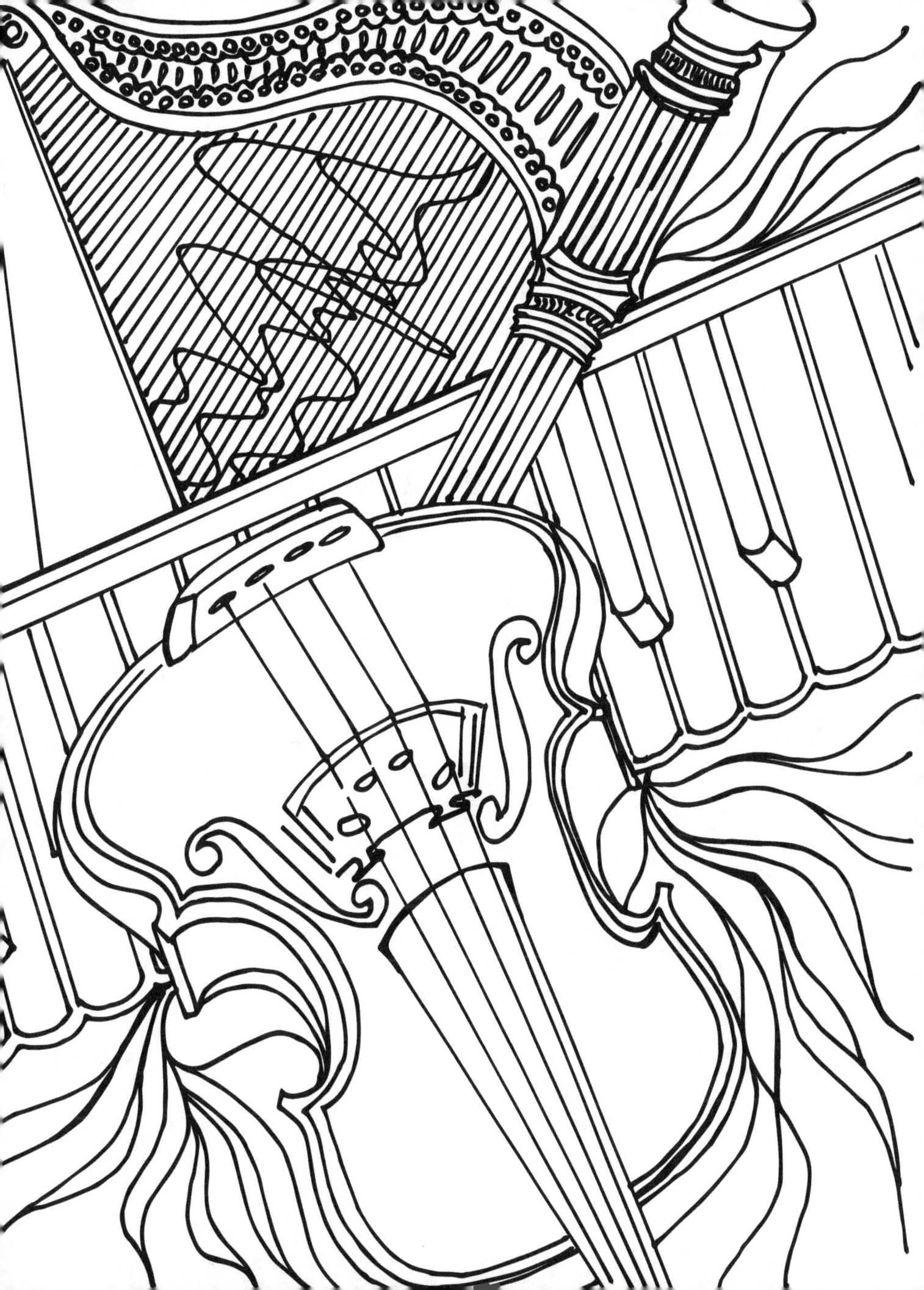

Consider color as a reflection of emotions.

Acid Jazz

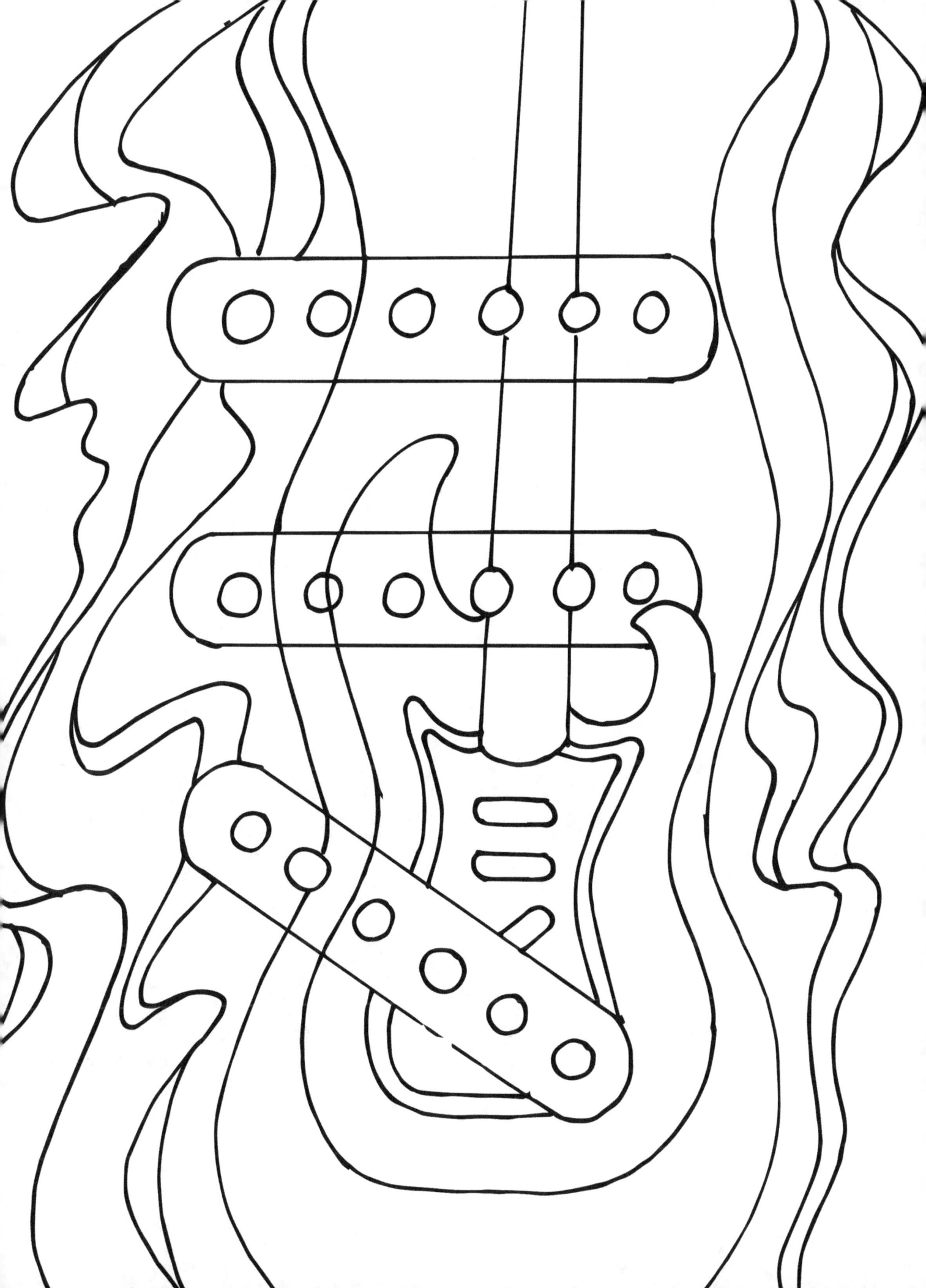

Music drives; art quiets.

Whammy Bar

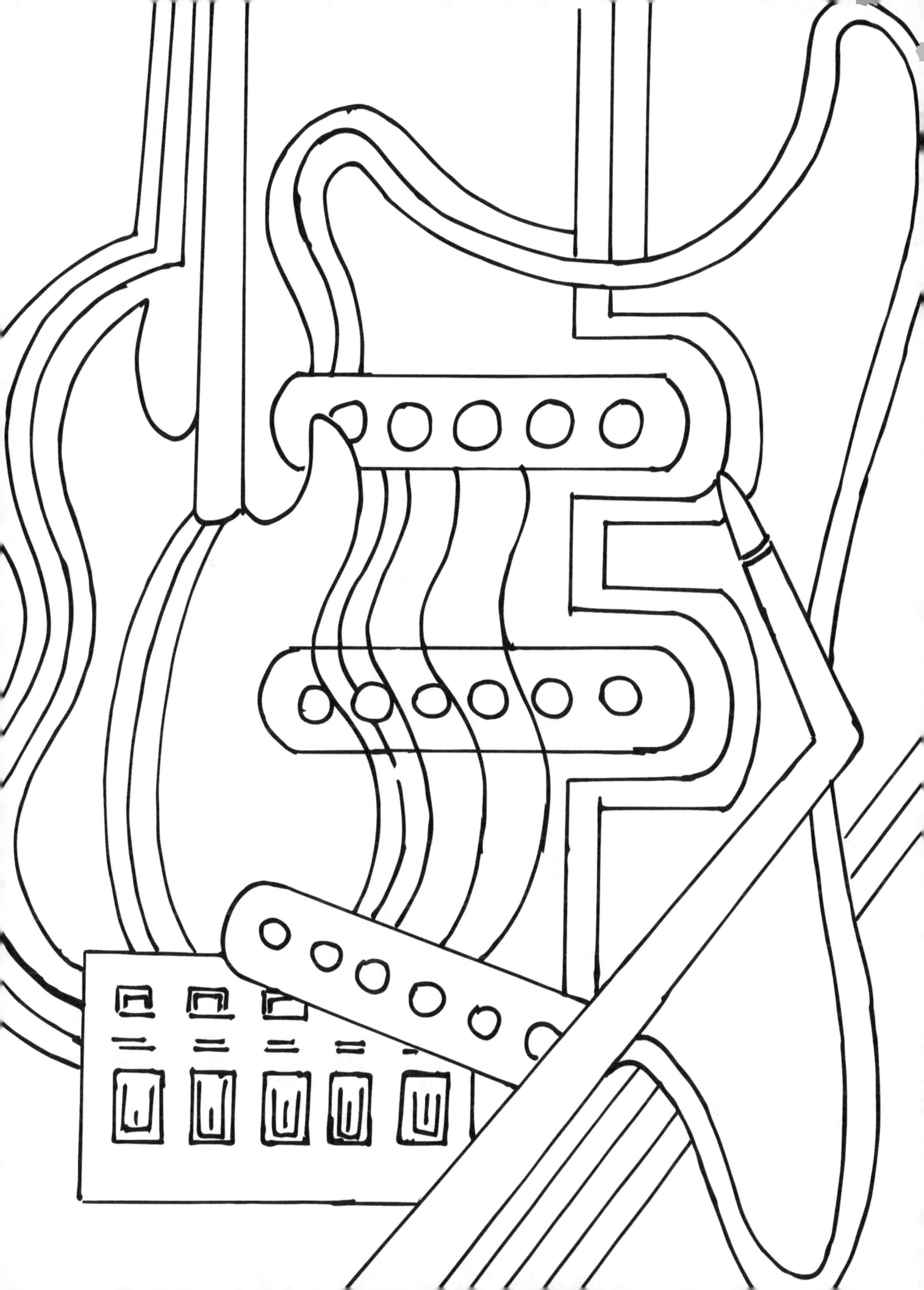

Express yourself in color.

Clarinet Symphony

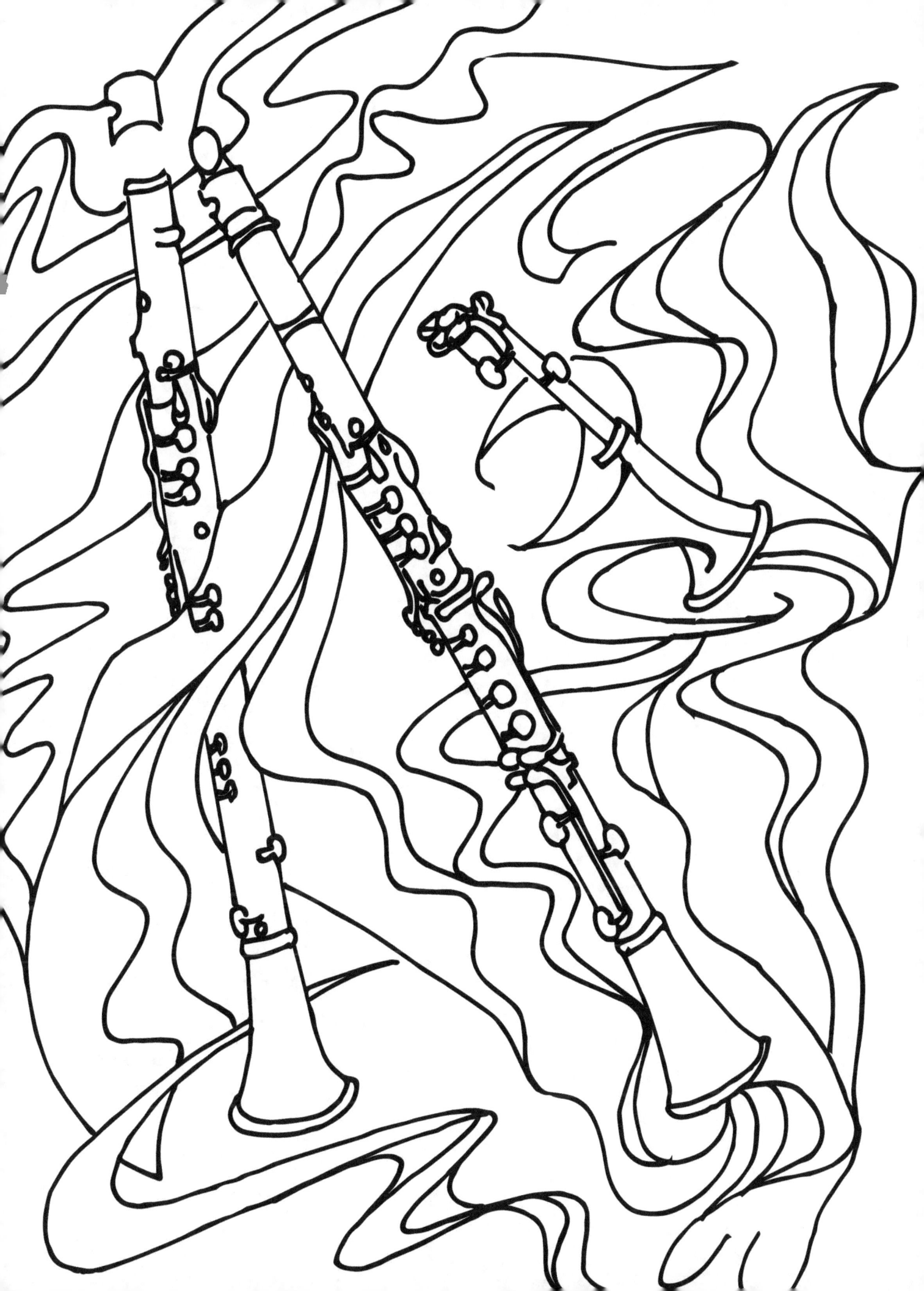

Sing it loud; sing it proud!

Brass Relief

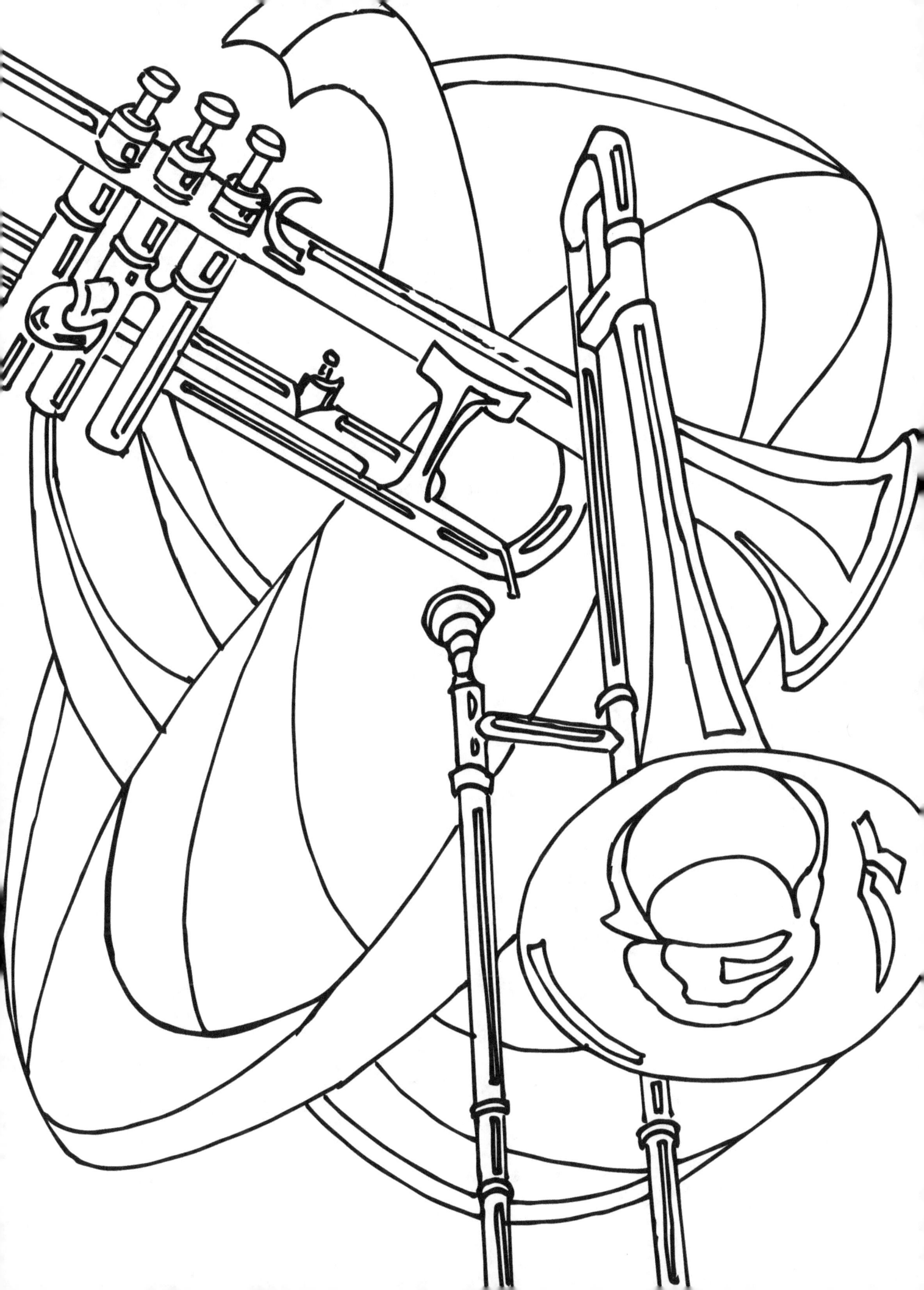

You're so sax-y.

Joy of Sax

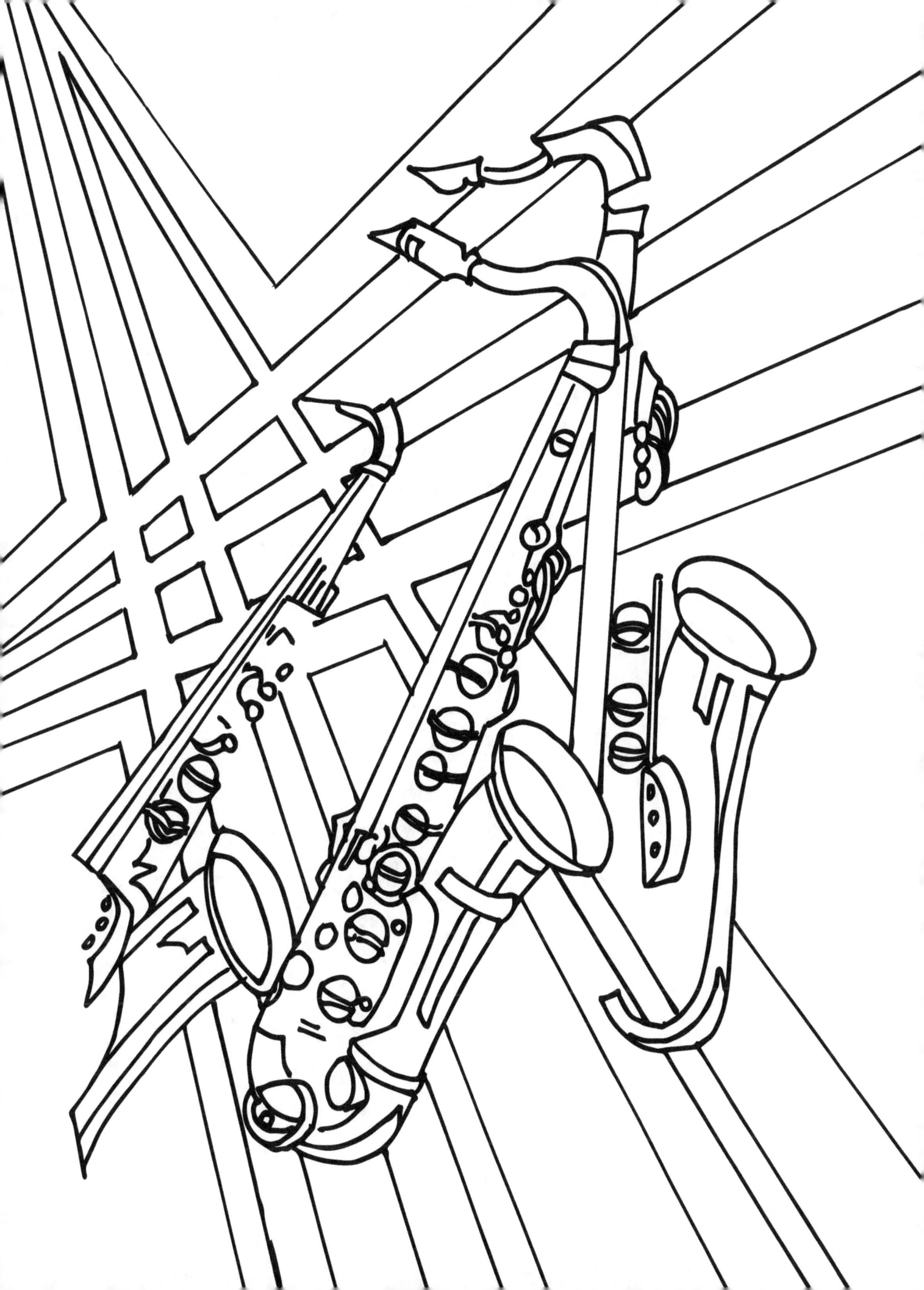

Music is the message.

Staff of Life Refrain

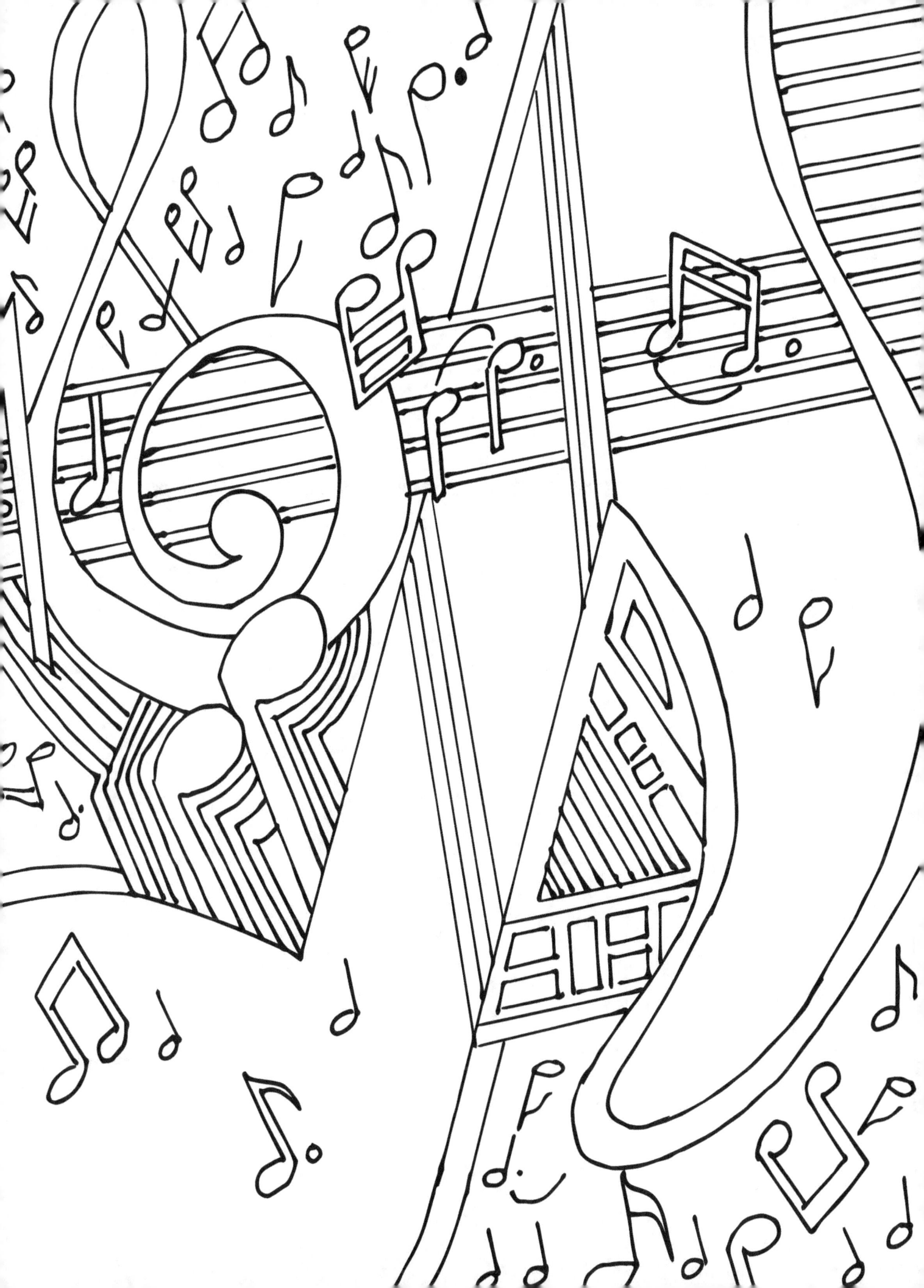

Always find time for the things in life that make you feel happy.

Body Art

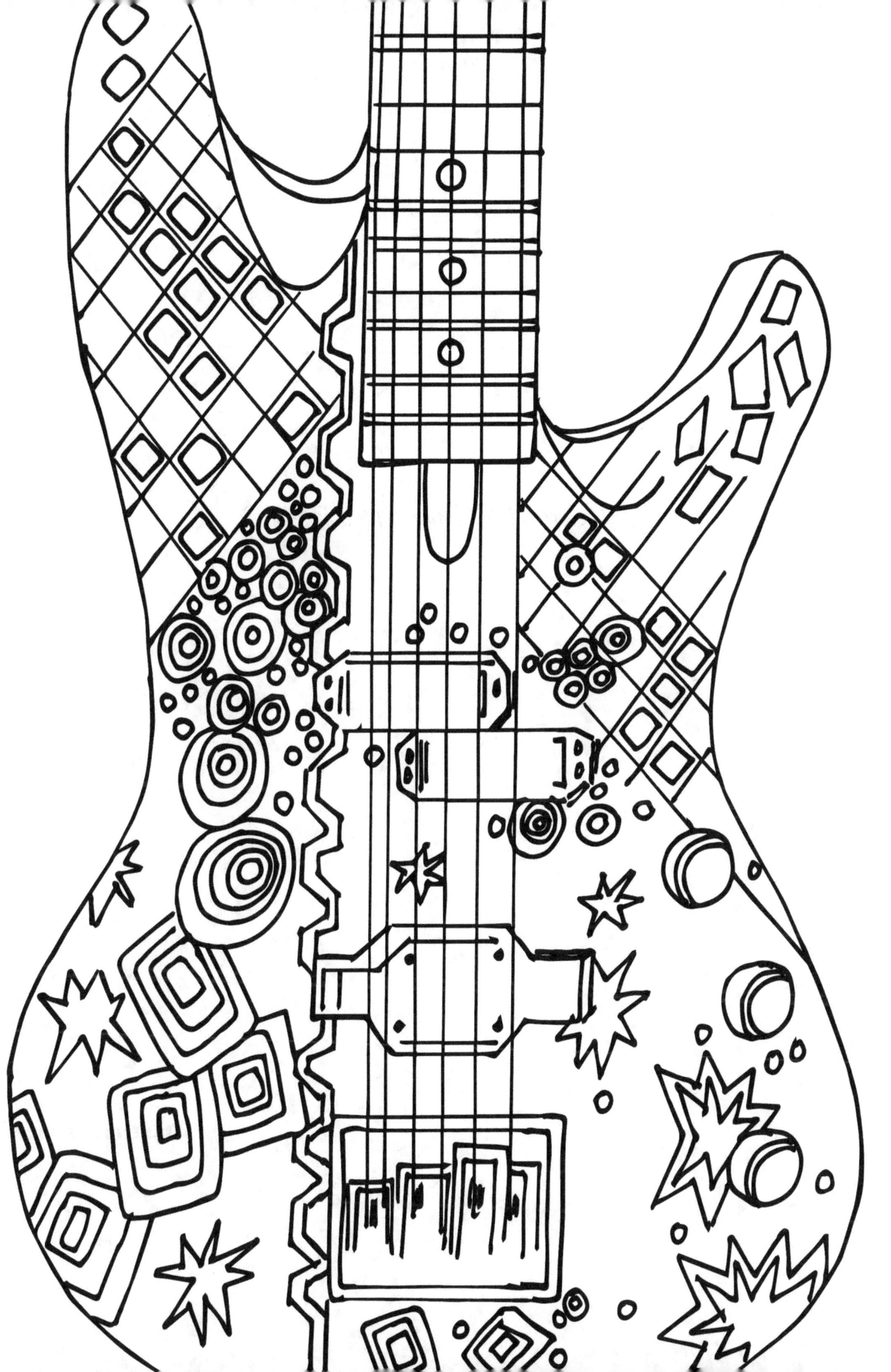

Color a little, dance a little, love a lot.

Electric Essence

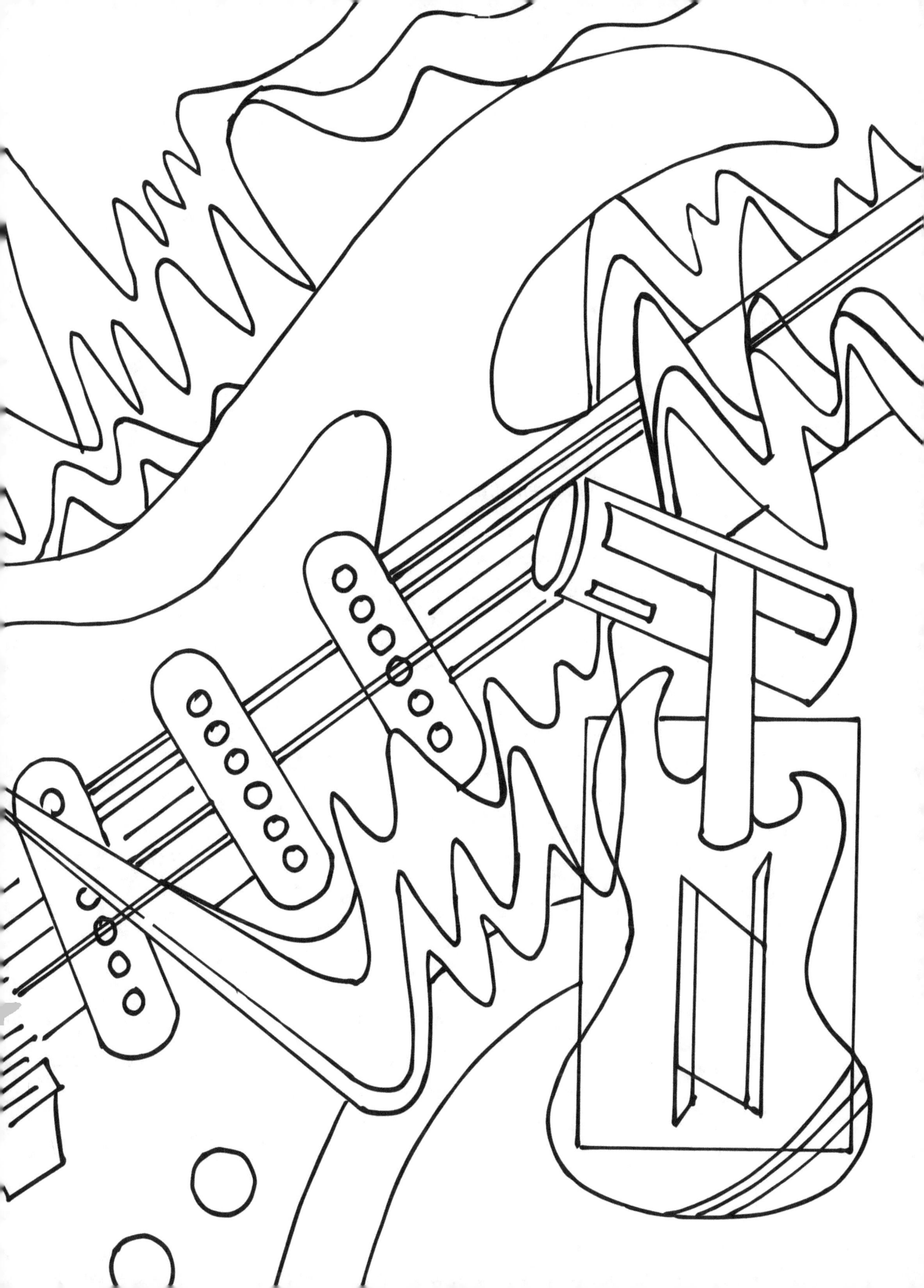

Rhythm –n- hues can brighten your life.

Guitar Parts

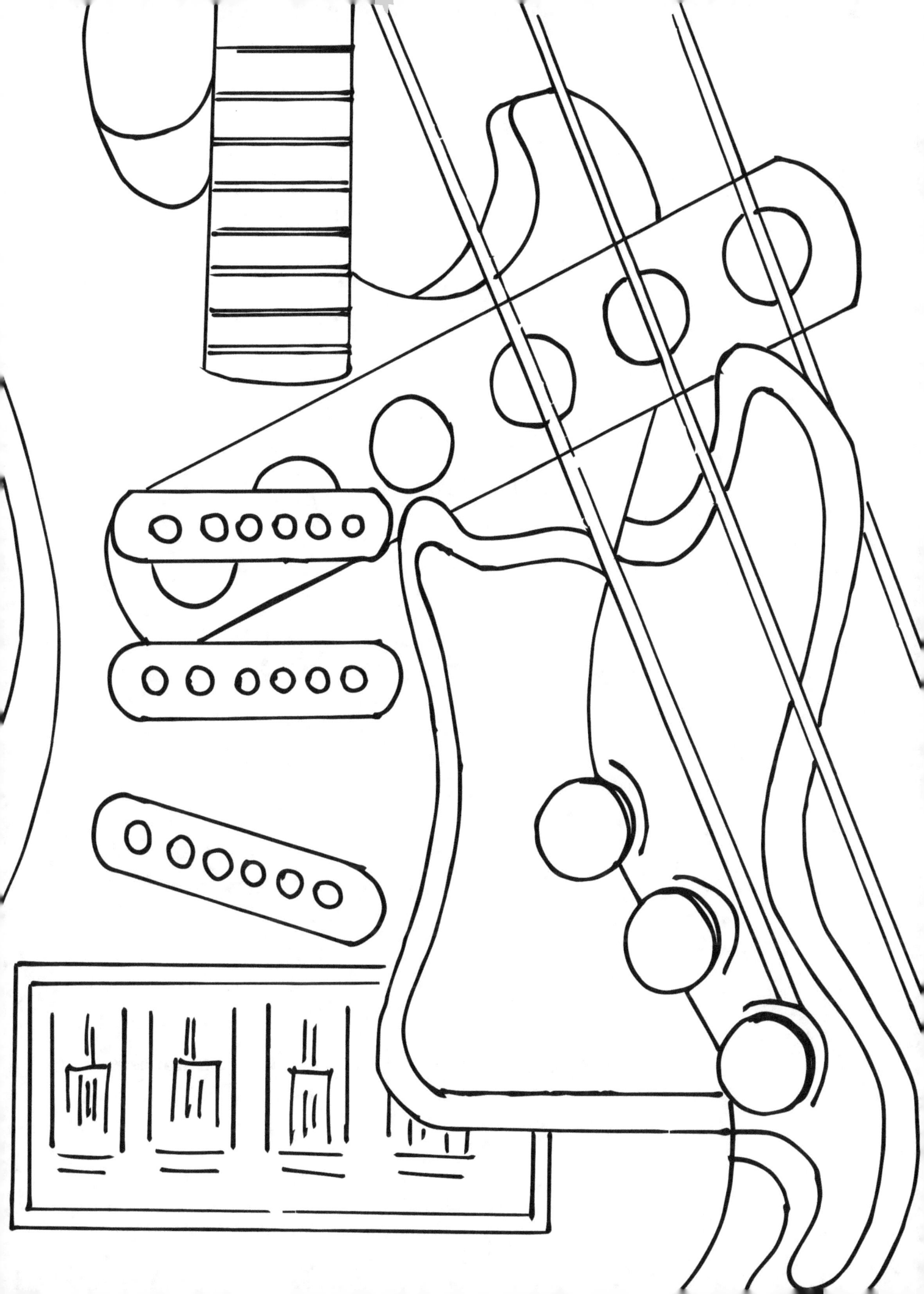

Feel free to express yourself.

Stratocaster Body

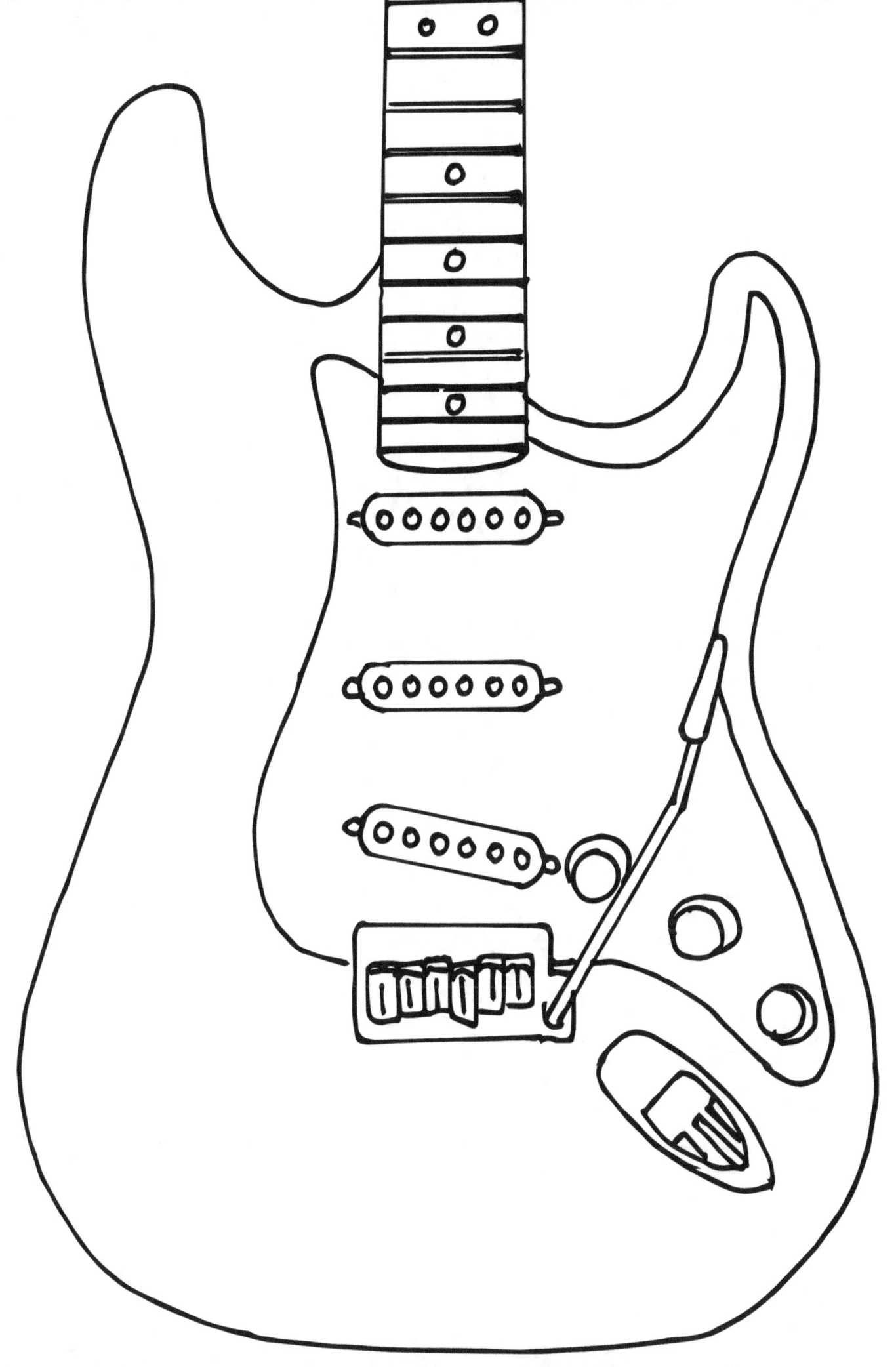

Be willing to be surprised!

Stratocaster Body

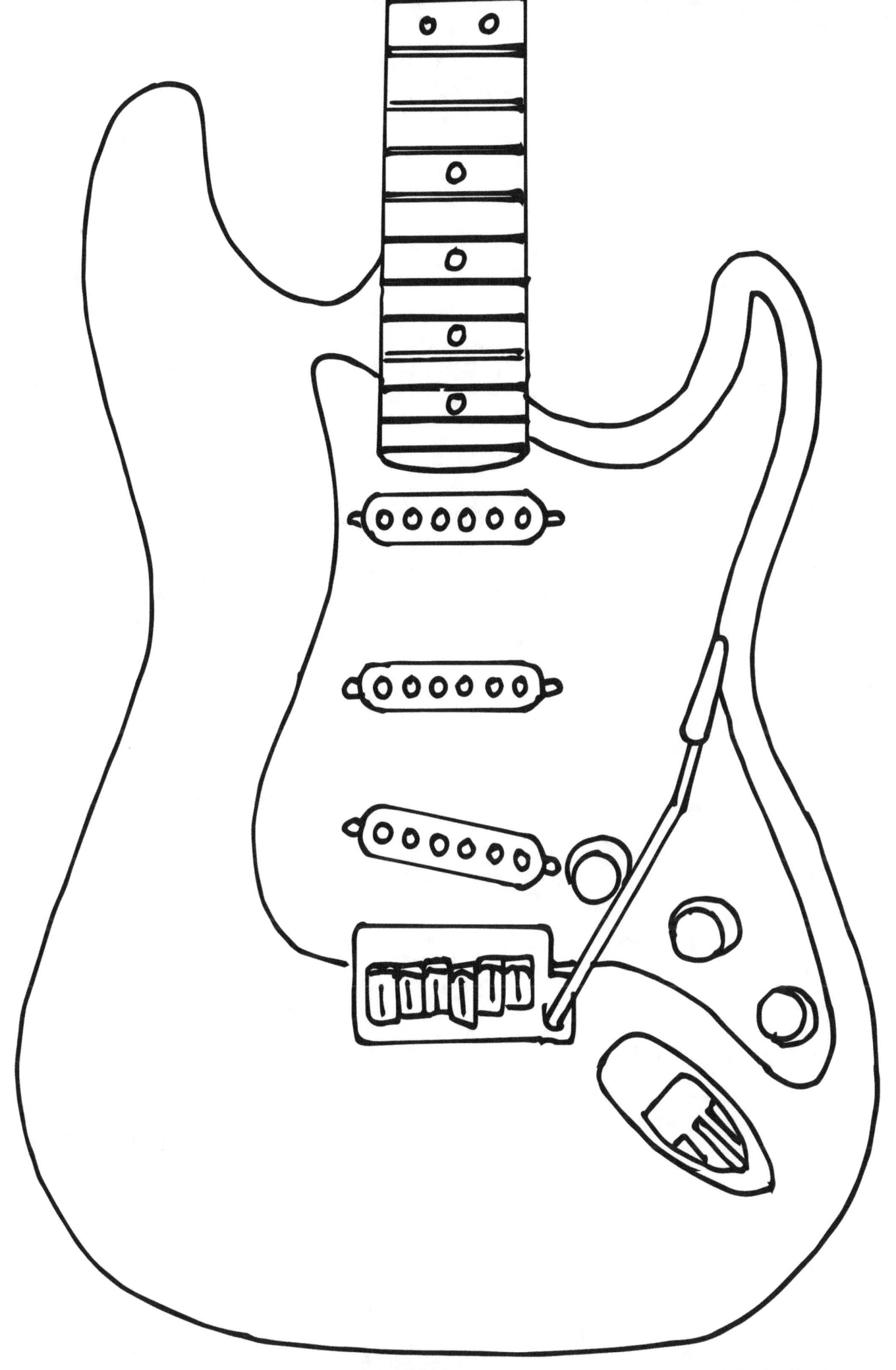

Color outside the lines!

Stratocaster Body

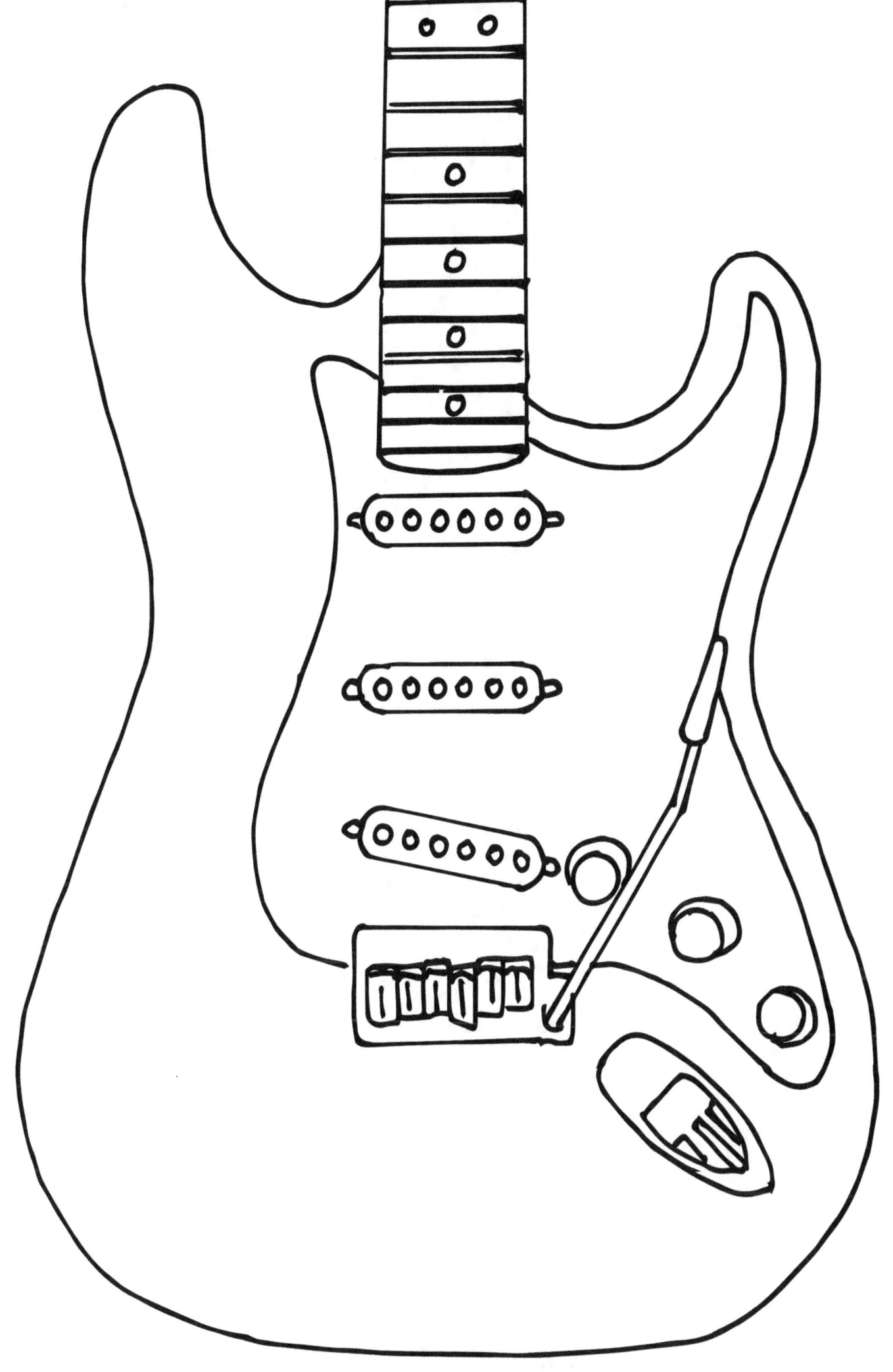

Doodles
Play on paper.

Notes
What's on your mind?

Doodles
Play on paper.

Notes
What's on your mind?

The Evolution of an Artwork

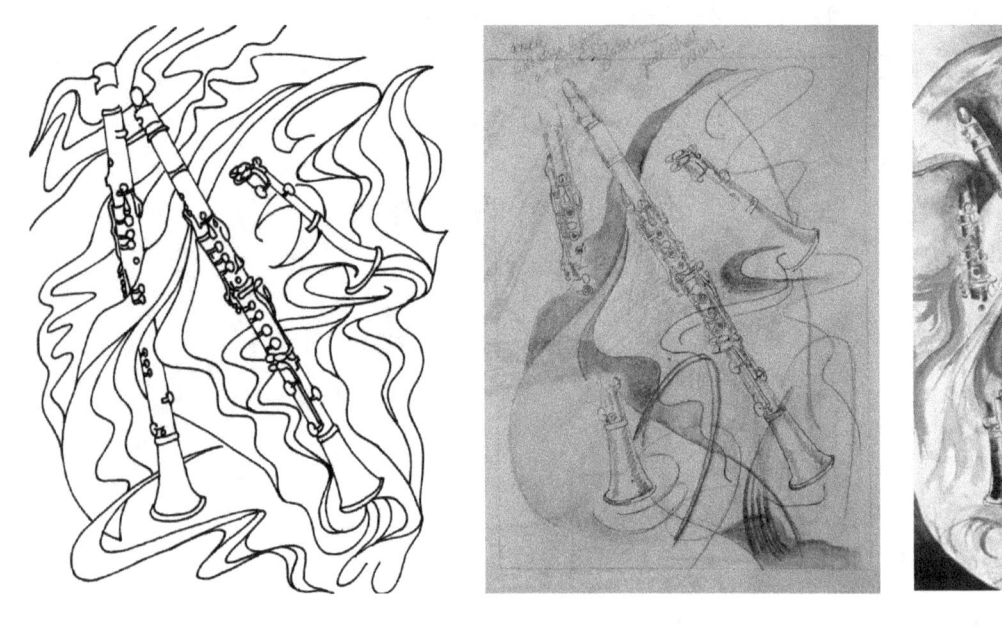

illustration   sketch   painting

See more artworks at www.rhythmnhues.com

Artist Biography

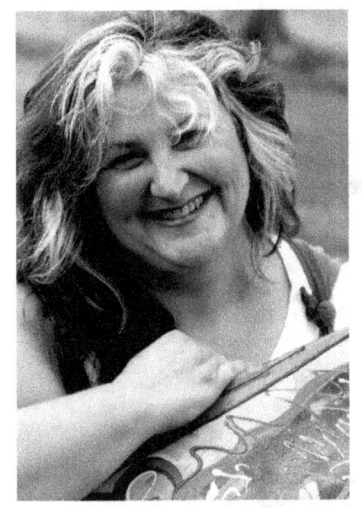

photo by Cathy Weems

Elizabeth Schafer creates musical compositions on canvas. Each piece is in the truest sense an improvisation, allowing the work to progress extemporaneously on its own — taking shape and coming alive filled with energy and expressed as the pure joy of sound through textures, line, shape and color; advancing and receding to form rhythmically constructed compositions on canvas. She has been on this harmonious journey for over 23 years, and her explorations have evolved along with her process which mirrors her approach to each series -- creating visual imagery of music and dance.

As a professional artist, Ms. Schafer's artwork has been showcased in over 70 solo exhibitions in galleries and museums, most notably in the Smithsonian Museum on Main Street Program, William Jefferson Clinton Presidential Library, Ohr-O'Keefe Museum of Art, and Meridian Museum of Art. She is a recipient of the Andy Warhol Grant, National Endowment of the Arts Grant, and Mississippi Arts Commission Fellowship Grant. Her public artworks can be seen in Art Across Arkansas, Thea Foundation in select locations throughout Arkansas; New Orleans Festival of Fins, New Orleans, Louisiana; Landfill Art Project, Wilkes-Barre, Pennsylvania; Mississippi Department of Transportation's Leo Seals Bay St. Louis Bridge, Bay St. Louis, Mississippi; and Time Whorp, Ohr-O'Keefe Museum of Art, Biloxi, Mississippi. Her works reside in collections at Florida Tech, Melbourne, Florida; Meridian Community College, Meridian, Mississippi; and Omni Royal Orleans, New Orleans, Louisiana.

Ms. Schafer is a member of the National Museum of Women in the Arts. She has been published in "Katrina, Reflections of Mississippi Women," and "Walking on Water;" and also appeared in the documentary film "The Art of the Storm." Additionally, she's been included in the following publications: Art in America, Art Gulf Coast, Where Magazine, and the New Orleans Times Picayune.

As a product of the 60's, Ms. Schafer was born and raised in the Mid-West in modest settings; surrounded by her family she gained her foundation and learned her sense of values. At the age of 18 she left the cornfields and headed south to the Florida beaches to seek out life's adventures and attend college. During her junior year of college, her mind filled with science and math, she sought out a mental break and found art in an adult art studies program at the Brevard Art Center and Museum. There she found her refuge and her passion. Shortly after graduating she relocated to the Mississippi Gulf Coast near New Orleans to pursue a career in oceanography unaware of the turn her life would take. It was there in the deep south where she began pursuing her life's calling as an artist as she discovered the layers of life and music along with her passion for painting.

Creating music-inspired art.

Let me see what you create!
Give me your feedback or tell me who you love to listen to while you color.

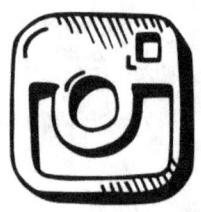

ArtbyLiz_Studio
#rhythmnhuescolor

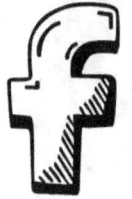

liz.artbyliz

www.rhythmnhues.com
www.artbyliz.com

contact@artbyliz.com

Share your creations with the world!

Exclusive limited-edition prints of these black and white illustrations along with original artwork and other prints are available for purchase on www.rhythmnhues.com.

More musically-inspired artwork is available online at www.artbyliz.com where original works of art focusing on blues, jazz, rock, and classical music are available for viewing and purchase.

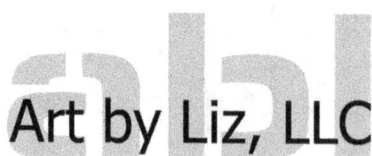

Art by Liz, LLC